What Made the Croco

What Made the Crocodile Cry?

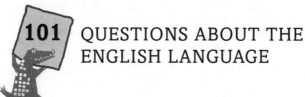

101 QUESTIONS ABOUT THE
ENGLISH LANGUAGE

Susie Dent

OXFORD
UNIVERSITY PRESS

OXFORD
UNIVERSITY PRESS

Great Clarendon Street, Oxford OX2 6DP

Oxford University Press is a department of the University of Oxford.
It furthers the University's objective of excellence in research, scholarship,
and education by publishing worldwide in

Oxford New York

Auckland Cape Town Dar es Salaam Hong Kong Karachi
Kuala Lumpur Madrid Melbourne Mexico City Nairobi
New Delhi Shanghai Taipei Toronto

With offices in

Argentina Austria Brazil Chile Czech Republic France Greece
Guatemala Hungary Italy Japan Poland Portugal Singapore
South Korea Switzerland Thailand Turkey Ukraine Vietnam

Oxford is a registered trade mark of Oxford University Press
in the UK and in certain other countries

Published in the United States
by Oxford University Press Inc., New York

British Library Cataloguing in Publication Data
Data available

Library of Congress Cataloging in Publication Data
Data available

Printed in Great Britain
on acid-free paper by
Clays Ltd, St Ives plc

ISBN 978–0–19–957415–5

1 3 5 7 9 10 8 6 4 2

Foreword

I love words and I love Susie Dent, so it seems right that I'm here writing the foreword for Susie's new book. Susie and I have known each other a long time, having been thrown into dictionary corner on Countdown together and it has been one of my favourite things to do since the very beginning. I have marvelled over the years at Susie's erudition and envied it.

I always wanted to be one of those people at parties who had the answer to random questions that crop up about the origin of words and phrases and often fantasised about slinging out perfectly formed, witty answers to peoples' questions, garnering admiration wherever I went. Alas, it was never like that. Like everyone else, I turned a blank questioning face to the enquiry, and wished that there was a little book I could keep at home, study it before I went out and impress wherever I went. And now there is such a book. Hurrah!

But many of you may not be as sad as me. You might be the sort of person who's just interested in words and phrases and doesn't feel the need to impress others with the length and breadth of your knowledge.

You will get as much, if not more pleasure, out of this book, because you won't feel the need to learn it off by heart like me. I've decided that in order to gain maximum advantage, I will learn some of the more obscure origins and then engineer it so other people ask questions about them and I can casually answer them.

So if you ever wanted to know why we have 'a whip round' or if you're 'a housewife' or 'a hussy', . . . or both even, this is the book for you.

For me, it's the bees' knees, oh 'crikey' yes. What 'serendipity', I'm going to put my 'bikini' on and get 'mullered'. Happy reading folks.

Jo Brand

Contents

Introduction

Curiosity famously killed the cat: an expression that comes high on the list of the most frequently posed questions about the origins of English. Not bad going for an idiom that in one form or another dates back to the sixteenth century.

But then so many characteristics of our language exert as much fascination today as they did hundreds of years ago. While usage, grammar, and spelling are the sources of our biggest bugbears, our greatest curiosity has always been individual words and expressions—their origins, their changes over time, their strangeness or beauty. But usage, grammar, and spelling can also intrigue. The questions English invites will never dry up simply because it is constantly evolving. Not for a single second in its 1,500-year history has English stood still, a fact that is as compelling to some as it is frustrating to others. Wherever you stand, whether you long for a linguistic golden age now passed or embrace today's new words with relish, the passion that English arouses is as strong as ever.

This book doesn't set out to answer the top 101 questions from a particular poll: certainly some of the standards are there—just what is a white elephant, why was Larry so happy, and who was Bob uncle to? (And what, while we're at it, is the point of that last Oxford comma?), but I have also included many of the riddles and curiosities that I didn't know existed before setting out, but which I then found irresistible. Why is it that only women get hysterical? Why isn't there a synonym for a thesaurus? Have there always been so many words in English for being drunk? And just who were flipping Ada and bloody Nora?

Questions about English are far from new. With the arrival of the printing press, those who needed to standardize a chaotic but wonderfully rich oral language must have deliberated long and hard over meanings and spellings. Shakespeare, coiner of so many words himself, will have pondered the stories behind the idioms and expressions he inherited. And with the arrival of William the Conqueror in 1066, Britons had to make hundreds of vocabulary choices as French began to hold sway over the incumbent Anglo-Saxon. Language, and particularly English, has never been a given. It has always been a choice, and a democratic one at that.

Some questions, of course, simply can't be answered. Those imponderables that I have included are there because, for me, their mystery seems itself to be in some way significant. We shall never know why cutting the mustard is a good thing (p. 10), but the journey of 'mustard' as slang is a near-perfect example of how the literal can jump the fence into all sorts of figurative terrains. If a 'geek' used to bite the heads off live chickens, what did the original 'nerd' do when it left the pages of Dr Seuss's imagination? Word detection is as open-ended as the objects of its study: some day we may discover the truth, but for now all the fun is in the educated guessing.

In the sixteenth century it was care or worry which proverbially killed the cat. Curiosity turned up some three hundred years later. But while an eagerness to know may have done for our feline companions ever since, it has clearly kept our language alive. As long as we puzzle over English, we nurture it, and the story behind the next new word or phrase will be just around the corner. A billion and one questions would never be enough to do it justice.

Susie Dent
October 2009

Acknowledgements

The final selection of questions that follow is of course subjective. I've tried to include a good cross-section of the linguistic conundrums (or conundra) that I am asked most often about, mixed in with some of my own favourites. But while the answers (and any faults that go with them) are mine, the starting points have mainly come from three sources. I thank particularly members of the *Countdown* audience, both in the recording studios and at home, who have found the time to send me the questions that have puzzled them for years, often decades. I am grateful also to readers of the *Radio Times* who have contributed some of the meatiest and most popular queries included here. Finally, hundreds of visitors to the *Ask Oxford* language query site posted questions that proved beyond doubt that English is in passionate hands. Although no individuals have been credited (the same questions were often put by a large group of people and it would have been unfair to credit only a few), if you will forgive the cliché, this book really wouldn't have been possible without them.

I would also like to thank Michael Quinion, whose word detection and expert riddle-solving both in his books and on his *World Wide Words* website have long been a tremendous source of information and entertainment, and John Ayto, another celebrated etymologist who has always managed to explain the most complicated linguistic and semantic journeys with a perfect common touch.

At OUP, Vicki Donald and Nick Clarke have applied deftness and expertise to the book's quick route through production. And Helen Liebeck has once more proved herself to be the copy-editor every author would wish for. Thank you.

Curious English:
The Whens, the Whys,
and the Wherefores

Why does English have so many terms for being **drunk**?

There are many hundreds of words and phrases for being **drunk**, not just in modern times, but also throughout the history of slang. A study by one of today's leading chroniclers of slang, Jonathon Green, of half a millennium's worth of collected material—amounting to almost 100,000 words and phrases—shows the extent to which the same themes recur. Back in 1938, one J.Y.P. Greig wrote in the *Edinburgh Review* that 'the chief stimuli of slang are sex, money and intoxicating liquor'. Factoring in the relatively new development of illicit drug-taking, together with the less openly celebrated bodily functions and a few choice insults, you have to conclude that Mr Greig had it right. Standard English has just a handful of words for being intoxicated. Slang, on the other hand, has over 3,000. In dictionaries of slang, drunkenness comes third in the number of terms that have existed for it over the centuries, after crime and drugs. Today, you can be **muntered, mullered, p***ed, slaughtered, blitzed, wrecked, trashed, plastered, sloshed, s**t-faced, wasted, bombed, canned, hammered, loaded, buzzed, smashed,** or **f***ed**. And that's just for starters.

The reason for such proliferation is probably born from the need for disguise. The role of slang has always been to keep others guessing. Its first role is to be a code that keeps those in the know in, and those who are not, out. As soon as the code is cracked and outsiders (often the authorities, especially parents or the police) scale the wall, then a new word is needed. Whether as an essential means of subterfuge in the criminal underworld (where Cockney rhyming slang began for just that reason) or as a marker of identity, slang is almost designed to be secret. It is a game that has been played for centuries.

Drinking has long been a habit that invites secrecy and euphemism, often mixed in with a good dose of humour. The eighteenth century saw a strong need to tiptoe around gin, creating a wonderful cocktail of terms in the process, including *diddle*, *sweetstuff*, *strip-me-naked*, *tiger's milk*, *tittery* (because gin makes you titter, an older term for 'totter'), *royal bob*, and the rhyming slang *needle and pin*, although *mother's ruin*, another euphemism of the time, certainly told it as it was. The term **three sheets to the wind** is at least as old as the early nineteenth century; it is a nautical metaphor suggesting that the drinker is 'top heavy'. The sheet harks back to the days of sailing ships, when it was the rope or chain attached to the lower corners of a sail and used to extend it, or to alter its direction. To have had **one over the eight** is to have had more than eight pints (i.e. a whole gallon), an excessive intake of alcohol.

Many terms go back much further still. The simple word **booze** has been around for over 500 years, while other very old terms compare a drunken person to an animal—to a newt, for example, or to a skunk or a rat. Back in ancient Roman times, the favourite comparison was a bit different—it was to a thrush. This seems curious, but it was probably quite common in the autumn months to see thrushes tottering around in the vineyards after eating partly fermented grapes that they had stolen from the vats. So familiar must this scene have been that the Romans created a verb meaning to be drunk based on *turdus*, the Latin name for a thrush. A descendant, many centuries later, in Old French, was the adjective *estourdi*, which over time changed from meaning drunk or dazed to violent or reckless. When English took it over, thanks to the conquering warriors, the violent and reckless invaders were the strongest, and so **sturdy** was born. And so even innocent words may have had a drunken past.

Whether euphemistic or dysphemistic (its opposite: in other words, plain rude), it seems unlikely that the lexicon of drunkenness will tail off any time soon.

Why do we call the short whiskers at the side of a man's face **sideburns**?

An American general of the nineteenth century, by the name of Ambrose E. Burnside, was immediately recognizable from his mutton chop whiskers and moustache, combined with (unusually) a clean-shaven chin. Thanks to his trend-setting, and from the 1870s onwards, people were calling this style a **Burnside**. The whims of fashion meant that the moustache was soon dispensed with as part of the Burnside 'look', and the term came instead to denote the strips of hair down the side of a man's face and in front of his ears.

Celebrity and fashion are equally fickle, however, and before long the general's name became rather opaque to the new fashionistas of the day. The 'side' element at least was obvious, but where did the 'Burn' come in? The first change made was to reverse the two parts of the term, so that Burnside became, in the 1880s, 'sideburns'. But this still left 'burns' a puzzle, and the more familiar 'sideboards' were substituted as an alternative.

A **beard**, by the way, is related to the Latin word *barba*, hence the word 'barber' for a hair-cutter. And **whisker** comes from the idea of 'whisking' or touching something very lightly, for a whisk (or 'whisker') in the fifteenth century could be a bunch of feathers used as a brush: the touch of that would probably feel very much like whiskers on your skin (in which 'board' simply means edge or border).

Two of my favourite expressions are **fair dinkum** and **bunkum**. Are they related?

In spite of their similarity these two wonderfully onomatopoeic words have quite different histories, and ones that set them miles apart geographically.

We all know dinkum, as in **fair dinkum**, to be Australian. In fact though, it was once very British, and originated as one of the wonderful dialect treasures that English has given us.

In the late nineteenth century, 'dinkum' meant 'hard work', or 'honest toil', and was often used among the miners in Sheffield and the surrounding mining areas.

During the First World War, 'dinkum' became military slang for a soldier, specifically one from Australia or New Zealand, which might explain why the word travelled across the oceans and took up residence in Australasia. For a while, there too, it meant hard or honest work, but that meaning faded from view over the course of the twentieth century. It survives in 'fair dinkum', that quintessential part of so-called 'Strine' vocabulary, where it can mean honest or straightforward—the genuine article.

Bunkum, meanwhile, used to be spelt 'buncombe', which gives us a clue as to its origin, for it refers to Buncombe County in North Carolina, USA. In around 1820 there was a furious debate in Congress as to whether to admit Missouri as a state in the Union, given that it still condoned slavery. Near the close of the debate, when the house was impatiently calling for a resolution, the Member of Congress for Buncombe rose to speak. Several Members gathered round him, begging him to desist; instead he persevered, declaring that the people of his district expected it, and that he was bound to make a speech for Buncombe. His speech was, by all accounts, both rambling and inconsequential. Hence 'bunkum' has passed into the language as a byword for nonsense.

Is it true that the precious stone **jade** was named after the physical cure it was thought to bring about? Were all jewels named in this way?

S ome precious stones are named after their colour (**ruby** goes back to the Latin word *rubeus* meaning 'red', while **onyx** comes from a Greek word for 'fingernail' because of the resemblance in colour between a nail and the stone). Others have more intriguing stories attached to their origin, such as **topaz**, which the Greek philosopher Pliny believed to have been named after an island in the Arabian Sea where it abounded. **Diamond**, meanwhile, the hardest substance ever known, comes from the Greek adjective *adamas* meaning 'unbreakable, very hard', and from it we have taken the adjective 'adamant'.

It is also absolutely true that many precious stones were thought to hold the cure to physical ailments. Books called 'lapidaries' (from *lapis* meaning 'stone') set out the wonderful properties of individual gemstones. Charles V of France was said to have had a stone that could alleviate the pain of childbirth, while the Duke of Burgundy was said in the fifteenth century to have had a ring with a gem that could detect poison. It was traditionally believed that putting an **amethyst** in your drink could prevent you from getting drunk (presumably you were not supposed to swallow it). The word, first found in medieval English, ultimately derives from the

Greek term *lithos amethustos*, the literal meaning of which was 'stone against drunkenness'.

Finally to the name **jade**, which surprisingly is not oriental in origin but European. It was believed in the sixteenth and seventeenth centuries that this typically green mineral could cure illnesses of the kidney. The Spanish word for the lower part of the sides of the body, where the kidneys are situated, is *ijada* or *yjada*, and so jade was named *piedra de ijada*, literally 'stone of the flanks'. Over time the *piedra* was lost, and the word came into English as simply 'jade'. The technical name for the mineral is *nephrite*, from another word, this time the Greek *nephros*, which again meant 'kidneys'.

Why do good things **cut the mustard**?

The word **mustard** has been used to mean something excellent or superlative for almost a hundred years—the phrase 'keen as mustard' draws on the same idea of added piquancy and zest. 'Hot stuff', in other words. In America, to say something was 'the proper mustard' in the early twentieth century meant it was the genuine article, and 'cutting the mustard' became a popular idiom to describe something that was up to scratch and more.

Like so many of our most intriguing phrases, the precise origin of 'cutting' the mustard has been lost over time, but for something that began as American slang the phrase now seems as quintessentially British as 'stiff upper lip' (also, surprisingly, American in origin).

Who was the first **toerag**?

The first sense of **toerag** in the *Oxford English Dictionary* is a quite literal one. A study of the typical life of a convict from 1864 includes the following description: 'Stockings being unknown, some luxurious men wrapped round their feet a piece of old shirting, called, in language more expressive than elegant, a "toe-rag"'. Some seventy years later, George Orwell uses the term in *Down and Out in Paris and London*, again in this literal sense even though the wearers had most definitely changed: 'Less than half the tramps actually bathed . . ., but they all washed their faces and feet, and the horrid greasy little clouts known as toe-rags which they bind round their toes'.

This straightforward meaning of a rag tied around the foot in place of a sock soon took on more figurative meanings including that of a tramp or vagrant, or, going further still, of a despicable or worthless person. It seems to have become popular within the circus: an 1875 account of *Circus Life & Circus Celebrities* notes that '*Toe rags* is another expression of contempt . . . used . . . chiefly by the lower grades of circus men, and the acrobats who stroll about the country, performing at fairs.'

The term **toe-ragger** is common in Australia and has the same meaning of a contemptible person. Some believe however that this has a quite different origin. The *Sydney Truth* newspaper reported in 1896 that 'The bushie's favourite term of opprobrium "a toe-ragger" is probably from the Maori. Amongst whom the nastiest term of contempt was that of *tau rika rika*, or slave'.

My Scottish uncle used to call me **corrie-fisted** because I was left-handed. I've never been able to find out where it comes from. Can you help?

There is a wealth of terms for being left-handed, and most of them are locally specific. Depending on where you are in the country, you can be **corrie-handed**, **Kerr-handed**, **kay-pawed**, **cack-handed**, and **caggy-handed**. Or a **cuddy-wifter**, **pally-duker**, or **southpaw**. Your uncle probably grew up with more terms than most. Within a fourteen-mile radius in Scotland there are fourteen different variations for being left-handed, and, what is more extraordinary, almost all have to do with the Kerr family from Ferniehirst Castle in the Scottish Borders. **Corrie-fisted** is one of them.

The story goes that the laird of the castle, Andrew Kerr, was left-handed, and he found it an extremely useful weapon in battle, allowing him to surprise the enemy with the unexpected direction of the sword. As a result, he only employed left-handed soldiers. The castle itself was built to maximize this advantage: whereas in most castles the staircases spiral clockwise, Ferniehirst has counter-clockwise ones, providing left-handed swordsmen with an advantage—the bends give a defender's left hand freedom to move over the open railing.

Given so many terms for left-handedness that equate it with clumsiness ('cack-handed' is just one), the Kerr family's alternative left-handed lexicon is a welcome relief.

I've been accused of being both a **geek** and a **nerd**. Does either word have a positive story to it?

I f we start with **geek**, I'm afraid the answer is categorically 'no'. In America at the turn of the twentieth century, a 'geek' was a performer at a carnival or circus whose show consisted of bizarre or grotesque acts, including, infamously, the biting off of a live chicken's or other animal's head. The word is probably a variant of the English dialect term *geck*, meaning 'a fool'. It was applied to overly diligent students in the 1950s who were considered a bit 'freakish' (the word 'freak' of course was also applied to live curiosities paraded at a circus), and to computer obsessives from around 1984. The story may yet have a positive ending, however: in the past decade, and like so many terms of insult, it has been reclaimed by the very people it is used against and worn as a badge to be proud of. The term 'geek-chic', born in the early 2000s, was the ultimate endorsement of this switch.

A **nerd** has more neutral beginnings. First recorded in the sense of a 'foolish or inconsequential person' in 1951, it seems to have been coined by Dr Seuss in his story *If I Ran the Zoo*:

> I'll sail to Ka-Troo
> And Bring Back an It-Kutch, a Preep and a Proo
> A Nerkle, a Nerd, and a Seersucker too!

Dr Seuss was using it as the name of an animal, and it is still not clear where the computer obsessive idea came from. The word detectives (often on the receiving end of both the 'geek' and 'nerd' labels) are still at work.

Where does the expression **by the skin of my teeth** come from? Do teeth have skin?

After Shakespeare, a prolific coiner of new words, the King James translation of the Bible has been the biggest source of phrases in English. **By the skin of one's teeth** is one of them. Meaning 'narrowly' or 'barely', and referring usually to a narrow escape from disaster, the phrase comes from the Book of Job, in which Job is subjected to horrible trials by Satan, to be relieved finally by God. The precise phrase Job uses is slightly different: 'My bone cleaveth to my skin and to my flesh, and I am escaped with the skin of my teeth' (19:20).

Exactly what the skin of one's teeth might be is not entirely clear, and there have been many theories put forward. The most plausible explanation is that it refers to the thin porcelain exterior of the tooth (rather than the gums). In other words, Job escaped with his teeth, but just barely. Job is comparing the narrow margin of his escape with the shallow 'skin' or porcelain of a tooth: the equivalent, in fact, of a 'hair's breadth'.

I know only two words beginning with 'syc-': **sycophantic** and **sycamore**. Are they related?

I ndeed they are. A **sycophant** is an insincere flatterer, one given the wonderful definition in the *Oxford English Dictionary* of 'a mean, servile, cringing, or abject flatterer; a parasite, toady, lickspittle'. It comes from a Greek word whose literal meaning was 'fig-shower'. The leap from one to the other seems a little hard to swallow, but a leap is exactly what happened.

Greek *sukon*, the root of the first part of 'sycophant', meant not only the fig as a fruit but also an obscene gesture, made by putting your thumb in your mouth. If you were a *sukophantēs*, you were essentially a maker of obscene gestures—in other words you 'showed someone the fig'. Over time, it is possible that the word came to be applied to people who informed on criminals to the authorities: perhaps, if we translate the thumb in mouth gesture into the modern equivalent, by putting two fingers up to the criminals and shopping them. There is one further possibility, which many believe, namely that a *sukophantēs* was specifically informing against the illegal exportation of figs. Wherever the truth lies, a sycophant was clearly as unpopular then as today.

One who grasses on someone else (a verb, by the way, that comes from the image of a sly and stealthy snake in the grass, although others conjecture that it is rhyming slang from grasshopper = shopper) will endear themselves to the authorities, and so *sukophantēs* became the term for someone who ingratiated themselves with the law. Eventually it became a byword for obsequious flattery.

The **sycamore** tree obviously keeps to the fig part of the equation: like 'sycophant', it has at its root the Greek *sukon* 'fig', and its Latin name is *Ficus sycomorus*, the fig sycamore.

Does the word **bankrupt** come from a literal breaking of a bank?

N ot exactly, although the theory is on the right lines. In the sixteenth century, moneylenders or traders used to conduct their business on benches outdoors. The usual Italian word for such benches was *banca*—hence today's 'bank'. A *banca rotta* was a 'broken bench'. In his dictionary of 1755, Samuel Johnson noted the common legend that when a money-dealer himself became insolvent, his table was duly broken as a sign to others. Whether or not this was true, *banca rotta*, which morphed into **bankrupt** in English, was definitely used figuratively to mean someone who had gone out of business—and indeed the modern sense of being 'broke' comes from that very same origin too.

My cousins talk of **riding croggy** for fun when they ride two-a-bike. Where does the term come from?

Contrary to what most of us believe, English dialects are alive and kicking. While many words (often regrettably) are dying out, new ones are being born, often the products of the young mixing up inherited vocabulary with the latest slang they use themselves. Yet some of the oldest words are still around today and have shown amazing resilience over the centuries, and it is often the most surprising subjects that have been the most enduring. Left-handedness is one (see p. 12), and children's games another. Within this last category, the fun to be had from riding pillion on a bike has spawned a wonderful medley of local words. There are dozens of local versions of sharing a ride on someone's bike. You can ride **backie**, **dinky**, **seatie**, **piggy**, and **croggy** of which more later. First though, why **pillion?**

The first people to ride pillion were on horses, not motorbikes or pushbikes, and they were not necessarily sharing the same mount. In the fifteenth century a pillion was a light saddle, especially one used by women. 'Pillion' is one of the earliest words to have entered English from Gaelic, where it meant a small cushion, but for its absolute beginning we need to look to Latin and the word *pellis* meaning 'skin'—many of the earliest saddles were made of fur or animal hide. The sense of 'pillion' to mean the 'seat behind a motorcyclist or cyclist' dates back to the late nineteenth century.

And so to 'croggy', which is still used in the Midlands—especially Nottinghamshire—and Teesside. The difference here is that the ride is on the crossbar rather than behind the rider. Believe it or not the word may have come north all the way from Cornwall, where a 'croggan' is a limpet shell: perhaps the idea is of two riders, one clinging tightly to the other like a limpet.

I've always been curious about **level pegging**. Where does it come from?

This probably entered the sporting lexicon from the card game of cribbage via the game of darts.

When darts first began to be played in public houses over a century ago, the absence of the digital counter you'd find today meant players used the pegs in an old cribbage board instead (cribbage is the card game where points are scored on a 61-holed board with pegs). When the scores were equal, then the pegs were level; hence the idiom **level pegging**.

The phrase **chalking up** also comes from keeping score, this time on a chalkboard or simply with a stick of chalk on an available surface. The idiom is surprisingly old: the *Oxford English Dictionary*'s first citation for it is from one of the Parnassus Plays, a series of entertainments performed at St John's College,

Cambridge, between 1597 and 1603: 'All my debts stande chaukt upon the poste for liquor'.

Finally, **tallying** and **keeping tally**, which can also be traced back as far as the fifteenth century, originated in the notching of a stick (the Latin verb *talliare* means 'to cut') as a way of entering a number.

Does **carnival** have anything to do with meat?

In Roman Catholic countries, a **carnival** was specifically the period preceding Lent, a time of public merrymaking and festivities. The word comes from a medieval Latin word made up of *carne*, which does indeed mean flesh or meat (as in 'chilli con carne'), and *levare*, to put away. In other words, it was the time to put rich food away for Lent. The same principle lies behind Shrove Tuesday (see **short shrift**, p. 36) and also Mardi Gras, a carnival held in some countries on that same day and which literally means 'Fat Tuesday'.

Men, Women, and A Few Things In-Between

Why do we call hooligans **yobs**?

Yob is a good example of 'back-slang'—a form of slang in which words are spelt backwards as a code so that others (usually parents) are unable to understand them. 'Yob' is simply 'boy' spelt backwards; the 'backward' element seems appropriate in the definition of retrograde behaviour.

Why is the adjective **hysterical** usually applied only to women?

Hysteria is defined in the *Oxford English Dictionary* as a 'morbidly excited condition'. Its linguistic origins show that it was once thought to be an exclusively female complaint. In ancient time, hysteria was thought to be caused by a disturbance of the uterus or womb. The English name comes from the Greek for 'womb', *hustera*, which is also the root of 'hysterectomy'. The German term for hysteria was *Mutterweh*: maternal suffering.

Hysteria was a popular diagnosis in the 1800s, when the medical profession used it to define female depression and nervous exhaustion brought about by societal pressures. Another name for hysteria was **the vapours**, so called because of the exhalations believed to come from the stomach and to cause all sorts of ills and ailments.

As men did not have wombs, they were inevitably seldom diagnosed with hysteria. The male equivalent, which displayed near-identical symptoms to hysteria, was **neurasthenia**, attributed to weakness or exhaustion of the nerves and originally seen as the direct equivalent for men to the 'hysterics' or 'vapours'. Later, as hysteria became a less fashionable diagnosis among psychiatrists and physicians, neurasthenia was applied to both sexes.

Even today, it is rare (and probably insulting) to hear of a man becoming 'hysterical'.

As a fan of the Errol Flynn movies from the 30s and 40s, I've often wondered about the word **swashbuckler**: was it someone who 'swashed' a 'buckle', and if so what on earth were they doing?

The traditional **swashbuckler**, described by the *Oxford English Dictionary* as 'a swaggering bravo or ruffian; a noisy braggadocio', was, indeed, someone who 'swashed his buckle'. To 'swash', in the sixteenth century, was to dash or strike something violently, while a 'buckler' was a small round shield, carried by a handle at the back. So a swashbuckler was literally one who made a loud noise by striking his own or his opponent's shield with his sword.

Errol Flynn also had roles as both a **buccaneer** and a **musketeer**. The origin of musketeer is quite simple: a soldier who fought with a musket. But a buccaneer may surprise. It originally meant someone who hunted wild oxen, because *boucaner* in French was to dry or cure meat on a *boucan*: a barbecue, in the manner of the Indians. The name was first given to the French hunters of St Domingo, who prepared the flesh of the wild oxen and boars in this way. This included hunters at sea: pirates who lurked off the West Indies, and so over time a buccaneer became a byword for a hostile sea rover.

Finally, it's worth mentioning the **Jolly Roger**. Some linguists believe this name for a pirate's flag, featuring a white skull on a black background, originated in the French words *jolie rouge*, meaning 'pretty red' for originally pirates used red flags as frequently as black ones. Supporting this theory is the fact that during the Elizabethan era 'Roger', was a slang term for beggars and vagrants and was also applied to privateers who operated in the English Channel. There are other theories too, including one plausible one that the term derives from a nickname for the devil, 'Old Roger': jolly perhaps because of the skull's grin.

Is it true that the words **housewife** and **hussy** are connected? Can I tell my wife that?

You can, but tread carefully! **Housewife** has gone the way that so many words describing women have gone: in that it went from a neutral word to one that for a while took on quite dubious connotations. A 'harlot' was once a court jester or buffoon hired to raise a laugh. And so it was with 'housewife' too: in the thirteenth century, which is the time of the *Oxford English Dictionary*'s first record of the word, 'housewife' meant simply what it more or less means today: a woman who manages the affairs of her household. Three centuries later it began to take on negative connotations of a light, worthless woman, even a promiscuous one. The *OED* has an entry from 1710 that reads 'There is . . . but An Hour in one whole Day between A Housewife and a Slut'. For a time negative and positive co-existed: Shakespeare was describing Nature as a 'bounteous housewife' at the same time as others were equating 'housewife' with 'harlot'.

For many centuries, **hussy** and 'housewife' were synonymous. A hussy was the mistress of the house. Like 'housewife', however, the term took on a sense of impropriety in the seventeenth century, even if with slightly more humour at that stage. Fascinatingly though, 'hussy' took on all of the bad connotations, as housewife lost them: the impudent promiscuous woman became a 'hussy', while the honest woman of the home retained the title 'housewife'. In the late nineteenth century, Ruskin was writing of 'the good housewife taking pride in her pretty table-cloth, and her glittering shelves'. In the same century, every soldier had a 'housewife' too, albeit of a slightly different kind, for the word could also mean a pocket case for needles, thread, etc.: it was probably this use of the word that bought into the idea of good housekeeping.

In the course of the twentieth century things changed again. 'Housewife' was a source of pride for mothers and wives for over 50 years: they were the homemakers. Twenty years later and feminism (often wrongly interpreted) denounced 'housewife' as a term that signified oppression and pigeonholing. Roseanne Barr famously said: 'I hate the word housewife; I don't like the word home-maker either. I want to be called Domestic Goddess' (as did, later, Nigella Lawson, albeit with her tongue in her cheek). Politicians and economists avoided the term: political correctness deemed 'schoolgate mum' and 'do-it-all' to be the appropriate terms and there have been a whole load of similar 'mum' spin-offs. Meanwhile, the popular TV series *Desperate Housewives* drew on the range of the word's associations, even if most people took the series, and the title, to be a pastiche of the wholesome American dream.

Like so many words used by and against women (such as 'bitch' and 'Jezebel', used by many a female rapper), both 'hussy' and 'housewife' may be in the course of being reclaimed and used with pride by women about other women. In the wrong hands, however, at least one of them remains high on the offence register. However etymologically correct, not every woman will appreciate that hussies and housewives were once one and the same.

Why should anyone want to **teach their grandmother to suck eggs**?

19

This curious idiom, said to those who presume to offer advice to others who are more experienced than themselves, is in fact one of many similar expressions which mean the same thing. Most of them date right back to the eighteenth century, and while sucking eggs has survived, other equally strange ones have not, among them *don't teach your grandmother to steal sheep*, and *don't teach your grandmother to milk ducks*.

Sucking eggs was a trick of thieves who broke into farms: they would surreptitiously suck the contents out of eggs on the spot rather than take them away and risk breaking them. The idea behind **don't teach your grandmother to suck eggs** is that an older person knows a lot more about cunning dodges than a younger one: their longer experience brings wisdom. An idiom which means the opposite, of course, is **you can't teach an old dog new tricks**, which associates getting older with a lack of flexibility and the ability or willingness to accept new ways of doing things.

One of the old legal texts in the chambers I work in describes a man as being a **buxom** member of a corporation. What can it mean?

Today's use of the adjective **buxom**, almost always applied to the female appearance, is a comparatively new one in the word's long history.

From the twelfth century, when the word can first be found, 'buxom' meant morally upright and obedient. The word was originally *buhsum* in Middle English, which meant 'easily bowed or bent'. The *Oxford English Dictionary* includes a quotation from 1380 from John Wyclif, the translator of the Bible from Latin into English in the late 1400s, which reads 'Oure Ladi Marye was buxumer to his bidding þan ony hond-mayde' ('Our Lady Mary was more obliging to his commands than any hand-maid').

This sense of compliance and meekness lasted beyond the Middle Ages until well into the nineteenth century; men too could be buxom. During that period the meaning began to shift little by little to one of amiability and kindliness, and from there it moved to being bright, cheerful, and lively. As good spirits depend on good health, a 'buxom' woman was soon one full of health, vigour, and good temper. Since plumpness has had a traditional association with health, a buxom woman was then plump or 'comely'. Particularly in certain areas.

Nubile, another adjective that now describes a young woman's physically pleasing appearance, may also surprise. A nubile girl, today one who is young and sexy, was originally simply old enough to marry, with no indication of attractiveness. The word comes from the Latin *nubere*, which meant to put on a veil and get married. *Nubere* is also the root of **nuptial**. And the ultimate root of all of these is the Latin word *nubes*, meaning a cloud—i.e. like a veil.

Why are French, Spanish, and Italian known as the **Romance** languages?

21

It is often assumed that these Latin languages acquired the attribute **Romance** because of their beautiful romantic sounds. This theory is true, in a roundabout way: it all comes down to the history of that word 'romantic'.

Historically, 'romance' means 'of Rome'. As the Roman Empire disintegrated, the Latin word *romanticus* ('of Rome') came to be associated with the languages that developed from the Latin of ancient Rome. By the time *romanticus* reached Old French, as *romanz*, it was being widely used to refer to stories in the local language, as opposed to *latinus*. Since many of these tales told of brave knights and their chivalrous rescues of fair maidens, resulting inevitably in love, the words 'romance' and 'romantic' took on the meanings they have today.

Is it true that the modern **gym** has something to do with naked men?

The first gyms go back some 2,500 years, where they played an important role in ancient Greek society. Gymnasia served both as training arenas for public games and as venues for socializing: people would go there to listen to lectures on philosophy, literature, and music. They were, inevitably, men-only affairs, and the word **gymnasium** reflects this. It comes from the Greek verb *gumnazein* meaning 'to exercise naked', and that is because athletes of the time competed in the nude as a tribute to the gods and in aesthetic appreciation of the male body.

Gymnasia sometimes hosted other, more spectacular, events too. Mock sea battles were among the most popular, for which the central arenas would be flooded. According to the historian Oscar Brockett, the most ambitious was staged in AD 52 on the Fucine Lake east of Rome; some 19,000 participants fought in it, and many of them died in the process.

I've always loved the sound of the word **berserk**. Where does it come from?

23

Berserk doesn't sound particularly English, although it has been in the language for over 150 years. For its ultimate ancestor we need to look to Iceland, and to the word *berserkr*, the word coined for a wild Norse warrior of great strength and ferocious courage, who fought on the battlefield with a frenzied fury known as the 'berserker rage'.

The word itself is made up of two elements. The second, *serkr*, was Icelandic for 'shirt'. *Ber* could mean one of two things. One sense is close to 'bare', and so the idea may have been that the warrior tore off his coat of mail and fought in bare-chested ferocity. The second, and more likely, translation, is 'bear', which may refer to a bear-skin worn by the warriors either in battle or before it as a ritual in the hope of absorbing some of the bear's fabled fighting prowess.

Whichever it is, few of us who blithely speak of someone going berserk today would think of the bare-toothed fury of ancient warriors.

Linguistic Prototypes:
How It All Began

What does it mean to **give someone short shrift**, and where does it come from?

The word **shrift** is a form of the verb 'shrive', which in the eighth century meant to give absolution (or forgiveness) of sins following the hearing of confession and the imposition of a penance by a priest. A convicted criminal would only have a short time to be given 'shrift'—be absolved of their sins—by the prison chaplain before their execution. Today, to give someone short shrift is to treat them in a dismissive way.

Incidentally, **Shrove** in 'Shrove Tuesday' is from the same root of doing penance. The day precedes Ash Wednesday and was traditionally the time when people went to confession in preparation for Lent. It is traditionally marked by feasting (especially on pancakes in modern times) before fasting begins.

What has the **bulldozer** got to do with bulls, or with them dozing for that matter?

25

The earliest sense of **bulldozer** had nothing to do with machinery. The original bulldozer was a bully who intimidated others. The word was spelt 'bulldose', and referred to a person inflicting a severe punishment and giving a heavy dose of flogging with a bullwhip: an enormous whip with a long heavy lash used for driving cattle.

The term 'bulldose' became very widely known during the US presidential election of 1876, which may have been the most hard-fought, corrupt, and rigged in the history of the Union. Historians say that Democrat supporters in the Southern states tried to stop black voters from putting in a Republican vote, shouting: 'Give me the whip and let me give him a bull-dose'.

A newspaper from that year (1876) wrote that '"Bull-dozers" mounted on the best horses in the state scoured the country in squads by night, threatening colored men, and warning them that if they attempted to vote the republican ticket they would be killed'.

Just a few decades later the word was used to describe heavy and forceful devices for pushing large items such as piles of earth or snow. What a leap from its beginnings to the bulldozers of today.

What did the original **lead-swingers** do?

To **swing the lead** is to shirk, idle, or malinger—in other words, someone who 'swings the lead' isn't pulling their weight. The sense goes back at least a hundred years and was certainly much used as army slang during the First World War. The one thing we do know about the term's origin is that it has a nautical theme. At sea, the 'lead' was a 'bob' or lump of lead suspended by a string in order to ascertain the depth of water.

The job of the leadsman was a difficult one, undertaken in often hazardous and extreme conditions. The modern sense of shirking seems a puzzling development, but one theory is that lazy sailors would simply swing the lead about rather than genuinely test the depth of the water.

There is another possibility though: an older military term, 'to swing the leg', also meaning to malinger (perhaps swinging the leg in idleness), may have been changed over time to 'swinging the lead'. We may never know for sure.

What does **cordon bleu** cookery really mean?

Someone who wants to produce food to the standard of haute cuisine might follow a **cordon bleu** course, a French name referring back to the 'blue ribbon' that, before the French Revolution, indicated the highest order of chivalry under the Bourbon kings. The *Oxford English Dictionary*'s first example of the term appearing in English is from 1727 and a quotation from Philip Quarll: 'He meets with several Noblemen, some with a blew Cordon'. The letters of Horace Walpole in 1769 include the expressive line 'Everybody rushes in, Princes of the blood, *cordons bleus*, abbés, housemaids.'

The term later began to be applied to other displays of distinction, and cookery was one of the first to take on the prestige of the blue ribbon. In 1827 a cookbook called *Le Cordon bleu ou nouvelle cuisinière bourgeoise* was published in Paris. Cordon Bleu cookery classes began in 1896, at Paris's Palais Royal.

Why do we **bury the hatchet**?

This phrase, meaning to end an argument or conflict, refers back to a Native American custom in the seventeenth century whereby a hatchet or tomahawk (the axe of the North American Indians, used as a weapon of chase and war) would be buried in the ground to signal the laying down of arms and the declaration of peace between warring groups.

Perhaps the most famous use of it in recent times was by the then PM Harold Wilson when he said of his Cabinet: 'I've buried all the hatchets. But I know where I've buried them and I can dig them up again if necessary'.

Why do we sometimes have a **whip-round** when we want to buy something?

A whip-round is a collection of money, usually taken for some informal purpose. The term has a long and varied history. A whip (or whipper-in) was originally a huntsman's assistant who kept the hounds from straying by

driving them back with a whip into the main body of the pack. ('Whippers-in', incidentally, first described today's parliamentary whips, whose duty it is to secure the attendance of members of that party on the occasion of an important vote.)

The literal meaning soon took on more figurative ones too, and to 'whip' could mean to encourage or force someone to do or feel something, such as 'whipping up enthusiasm' for a cause. A slang dictionary of 1865 explains a further meaning of the noun 'whip' in officers messes: 'after the usual allowance of wine is drunk . . . those who wish for more put a shilling each into a glass handed round to procure a further supply'. Just nine years later the term 'whip-round' took over as the more usual word for this kind of money collection in the army, and before long crossed over into civilian life too.

When were the first **ploughman's lunches** eaten?

A **ploughman's lunch** of bread, a good hunk of cheese, some pickle, and perhaps pickled onions, is a regular on today's pub menus. But did ploughmen ever eat them?

Packed lunches are a common part of life, whether in the office, car, school playground, or building site. Surprisingly however, there doesn't seem to be any great regional variation or even any great variation at all in the way the portable meals we eat are described. We are eating a **packed lunch**, perhaps a **pack lunch**, or in North America sometimes a **sack lunch**. Rural labourers in the field did, however, eat something quite specific when they opened their bags in the late morning. They still do; it's just that there aren't so many of them now. Two main trends are visible in what these people ate. Some names are literal, referring directly to food (e.g. *drinkings*, *morsel*, *sup-and-a-bite*) or to the fact of the food being packed (e.g. *bagging*, *packing*). More interesting are the array of terms which refer to the time when the meal was taken, from specific times like *eleveners* (what we now usually call 'elevenses'), *nineses*, and *ten o'clock*, through general references to time (*clocking*, *clocks*), to those where the time in question, usually noon, is concealed in the first syllable (*nuncheon*, *nummit*).

One thing those labourers didn't eat, even the ploughmen it seems, was a ploughman's lunch. The earliest description of one in the *Oxford English Dictionary* is not until 1957 in the *Monthly Bulletin* of the Brewers' Society: 'There followed a "Ploughman's Lunch" of cottage bread, cheese, lettuce, hard-boiled eggs, cold sausages and, of course, beer'.

That is not to say that a ploughman would not have had some of these things, especially bread and cheese, in his 'nummit' (a contraction of 'noon-meat') or 'clocking': he just didn't call it that. We have cheese marketers to thank for that.

I know the **bikini** was named after the Bikini atoll, but what is the connection?

In 1946 the USA exploded an atom bomb at Bikini in what was known as the Castle Bravo nuclear test. Bikini was an atoll (a circular reef) in one of the Micronesian Islands in the western Pacific, part of the Republic of Marshall Islands. It was the site for over twenty nuclear tests by the USA in the period between 1946 and 1958.

Just days after the first nuclear test was carried out on the atoll, a scanty two-piece swimming costume caused a sensation on the beaches of France. Described as 'the smallest bathing suit in the world' that could 'split the atom', its effect was said to be so powerful that the French dubbed it the **bikini** in allusion to the dramatic effect of a nuclear explosion.

The term 'bikini' seems to have appeared first in English in an American newspaper, the *Waterloo Daily Courier*, in 1947. It reported: 'The French, it seems, have a new suit planned that is about twice as wide as a piece of string. It's so explosive that they call it the Bikini.' Three years later the *News of the World* reported that an unnamed woman 'made an unsuccessful attempt yesterday to swim in a Hampstead Heath pond in her home-made "Bikini" costume'.

And so the bikini arrived on British shores, soon to be made unforgettable by the bombshell Ursula Andress in *Dr No*. (A

bombshell, before the term was applied to a dramatically unexpected event or a sexy woman, was originally the casing of the very first bombs.)

Incidentally a **blockbuster**, which of course now means a great commercial success, was in the 1940s a huge aerial bomb capable of destroying a whole block of streets.

Why do we talk about **stealing someone's thunder**?

T his idiom, defined as using the ideas devised by another person for your own advantage, has a gratifyingly literal story behind it.

It is quite rare for etymologists to pinpoint the very first use of a word or phrase. In this case, however, the eighteenth-century actor and playwright Colley Cibber, in his *Lives of the Poets*, recounted the exact events that spawned the idea of 'stealing thunder'. Alexander Pope also mentioned them in his poem *The Dunciad*. The story they tell involves a man called John Dennis, an actor-manager of the early part of the eighteenth century who had invented a machine that reproduced for the stage the sound of thunder.

Dennis used his invention for the first time in his own play, *Appius and Virginia*, performed at Drury Lane Theatre in London in

1709. By all accounts Mr Dennis's writing skills did not match his creative ones, and his play closed after a short run, to be replaced by a production of *Macbeth* performed by another company. Dennis himself went along to the opening night and was outraged to hear his thunder machine being used. The story goes that he stood up and shouted, 'Damn them! They will not let my play run, but they steal my thunder.'

The phrase seems to have taken a while to enter the language figuratively. The *Oxford English Dictionary*'s first example of its use is as late as 1900. It is likely, though, that it was used in conversation and particularly within theatrical circles long before then.

Where does the phrase **in a nutshell** come from?

This idiom, used when we want to sum something up in a concise way, goes back over four hundred years to the late sixteenth century—Shakespeare's Hamlet uses it to mean something compact when he says, 'I could be bounded in a nutshell, and count myself a king of infinite space, were it not that I have bad dreams'.

The phrase originates in an ancient story, described by the Roman scholar Pliny in AD 77, that the great philosopher Cicero witnessed a copy of Homer's epic poem the *Iliad* written on a piece of parchment that was quite small enough to fit into the shell of a walnut.

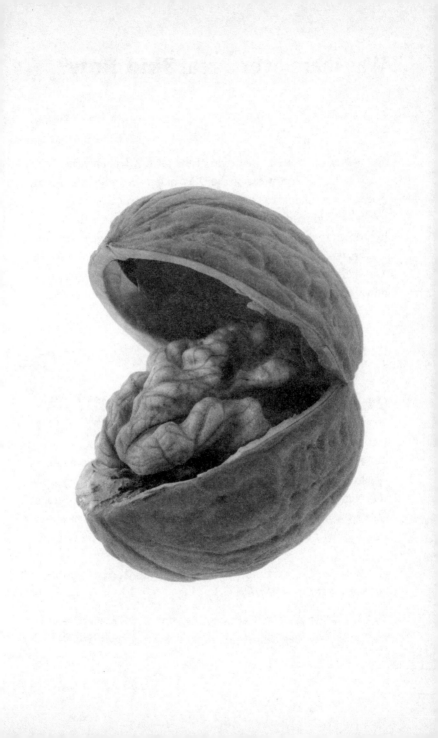

Was there ever a real **Skid Row**? 34

Yes, there was. The origin of the term is probably the Pacific Northwest of the USA: one place in Seattle, Yesler Way, claims to be the first skid row. It was a sloping track—a 'skid road'— that was used by timber workers to slide logs down to the lumber mills. Once the heavy work was over, the loggers would congregate in the cheap bars in the area after work. The skid road turned into **Skid Row**, now used to mean any run-down area of a town where people on the down and out gather.

Where does the term **gerrymandering** come from? 35

In political contexts, **gerrymandering** is the manipulation of the boundaries of electoral districts to give an advantage to a particular party or class. The term was coined when Elbridge Gerry, the governor of Massachusetts in 1812, created a new voting district that appeared to favour his Democratic party.

The Memorial History of Boston, published in 1881, reported the birth of the term as follows:

'In 1812, while Elbridge Gerry was Governor of Massachusetts, the Democratic Legislature, in order to secure an increased representation of their party in the State Senate, districted the State in such a way that the shapes of the towns forming such a district in Essex county brought out a territory of regular outline. This was indicated on a map which Russell the editor of the "Continent" hung in his office. Stuart the painter observing it added a head, wings, and claws, and exclaimed "That will do for a salamander!" "Gerrymander!" said Russell, and the word became a proverb.'

The Gerrymander was further cemented in the language when the *Boston Weekly Messenger* published a cartoon of a map embellished with claws, wings, and fangs.

Gerrymandering created some odd-looking districts. They included the Monkey-Wrench district of Iowa, the Dumb-Bell district of Pennsylvania, the Horseshoe district of New York, and the Shoestring district of Mississippi.

Serendipity often tops the polls of the nation's favourite words. But where does it come from?

36

The wonderfully onomatopoeic **serendipity**, which is indeed often chosen as Britons' favourite English word (alongside 'nincompoop' and 'discombobulate'), means the making of happy and unexpected discoveries by accident. It was invented by the writer and politician Horace Walpole in 1754 as an allusion to **Serendip**, an old name for Sri Lanka. Walpole was a prolific letter writer, and he explained to one of his main correspondents that he had based the word on the title of a fairy tale, *The Three Princes of Serendip*, the heroes of which 'were always making discoveries, by accidents and sagacity, of things they were not in quest of'.

Incidentally, the original Persian name for Sri Lanka (and in earlier times Ceylon) was *Sarandib*, a corruption of the Sanskrit *Sinhaladvipa* which literally meant 'the island where lions dwell'. Sinhalese is still the name for the most commonly spoken Sri Lankan language.

Words on Show

Why are actors in background roles supposed to say '**rhubarb, rhubarb**' for the sound of inaudible chatter?

'**Rhubarb**' was originally thought of as a foreign or 'a strange' plant from unkown shores. The word rhubarb goes back to the Latin word *rhabarbarum*, the second part of which comes from Greek *barbaros* meaning 'foreign' (hence 'barbarian', which acquired its meaning of someone savage and uncivilized because the Greeks thought all foreigners spoke in a strange and completely unintelligible tongue that sounded to them like 'ba ba ba'). In the same way, actors who wanted to give the impression of indistinct background conversation on stage traditionally achieved this by repeating 'rhubarb, rhubarb'.

Why is the reception room in a theatre or TV studio known as the **green room**?

The theatre is packed full of wonderful terms. The **green room** is one of the most curious. Originally, the term referred to an off-stage room in a theatre where actors could rest while they were waiting for their cues. Today it is where performers or interviewees gather before their turn.

Why it should be called a green room is a bit of a mystery. The first mention that the *Oxford English Dictionary* can find is in a play first performed in London in 1701, when it seemed simply to suggest a green-painted room. One suggestion is that the colour green rested the actors' eyes after performing with bright stage lighting.

Another theory is that the colour green has long been associated with the theatre, perhaps originating in the liveries worn by members of acting companies in the time of Shakespeare. Green baize was also sometimes used to cover the stage at this period to protect the costumes of the actors. 'The green' has also been a term for the stage itself since around the 1940s, originating in the rhyming slang greengage = stage.

Did anyone ever **explode onto the scene** for real in theatres gone by?

They did, but not in the sense you might expect. For the citizens of ancient Rome, **exploding** was something you did to an actor in the theatre if their performance was not up to scratch. The word is made up of two Latin forms, *ex* and *plaudere*. The *ex* prefix meant 'out', while *plaudere* was a verb meaning to clap (hence today's 'applaud'). So to 'explode' was literally to drive someone off the stage by clapping or hissing.

Over time, the verb lost its literal application and was used figuratively to mean rejecting something or someone quite forcefully, or to disapprove. Today, to 'explode' a theory or idea is to disprove it irrefutably. How did dynamite and bombs come into the frame, as they did in the late 1800s? They are probably an extension of the idea of a loud noise that once accompanied the forcing of an actor off the stage.

Where does the expression **playing to the gallery** come from?

Galilee, the northern region of ancient Palestine where Jesus is said to have lived and travelled, is probably the ultimate source of **gallery**, which entered English from the Italian word *galleria*, a church porch. The word was probably an alteration of *galilea*, 'galilee', which was used as the name for a chapel or porch at the church entrance. The idea behind this was probably that the porch was at the end of the church furthest away from the altar, just as Galilee, an outlying portion of the Holy Land, was far from Jerusalem.

From the mid-seventeenth century the highest seating in a theatre was called the gallery, and this was where the cheapest seats—and the least refined members of the audience—were found. Hence, **to play to the gallery**, an expression dating from the late nineteenth century, is to act in a showy or exaggerated way to appeal to popular taste.

Why must actors never utter '*Macbeth*' in the theatre, but call it 'the Scottish Play' instead?

There are numerous theories behind this long-held superstition. Productions of *Macbeth* are said to have been plagued with accidents, many ending in death. One story links this back to the original performance of the play, in which prop daggers were said to have been mistakenly swapped for real ones, resulting in a fatal accident.

Another belief is that the curse of *Macbeth* has been cast by the three Witches of the play, who represent darkness, chaos, and evil, some believe are exacting revenge against Shakespeare himself for using spells he took from an actual coven of witches in the writing of the tragedy.

The most likely explanation is, as so often, rather more mundane. The superstition probably arose at a time when many theatres were in danger of going out of business due to decreasing audiences. In an attempt to stay afloat, they might well have announced the production of a true crowd-pleaser, which *Macbeth* certainly was. Nonetheless, in the toughest of climates, even that play may not have proved enough to save the company, in which case *Macbeth* may have presaged the end of a company's season and of the closure of the theatre itself. Over time, *Macbeth* may then have become synonymous with bad luck.

Today, when the name of the play is spoken in a theatre, tradition requires that the person must leave, perform one of a number of rituals, and be invited back in. These traditional rituals, said to ward off evil when the play is mentioned, include turning round three times, spitting over one's left shoulder, swearing, or reciting a line from another of Shakespeare's plays. This was parodied in an episode of *The Simpsons*, when Sir Ian McKellen was struck by lightning after saying the play's name.

The Blackout Crew recently put out a song out with the title 'Put a Donk On It'. What is a **donk**?

42

The *Oxford English Dictionary*'s first record of **donk** is from 1916, where it is a colloquial abbreviation of 'donkey'. It's unlikely that the Blackout Crew song has anything to do with a four-legged animal, however. According to the democratic slang lexicon that is *urbandictionary.com*, it can mean either a sound-placed midway between beats in house music, or a rounded and attractive bottom. The Blackout Crew is (probably) referring to the latter. Incidentally, the donk in the song is also declared to be 'sick'! **Sick** here is the latest in a very long line of words of approval; once a part of surfers' slang, in which a 'sick wave' was the ultimate goal, it is now very much part of the teen repertoire for 'cool'.

Who was the fat lady whose song meant the end of something?

It ain't over till the fat lady sings is a well-worn phrase used to reassure someone that there is still time for something good to happen. It is to be found particularly in sport as a message of consolation to the losing team in the course of a championship, and is often attributed to Yogi Berra, the former Major League Baseball player and manager whose witticisms are well known (such as 'Half the lies they tell about me aren't true,' 'The future ain't what it used to be,' and—one which sounds very much like the phrase in question—'It ain't over till it's over').

Certainly the first quote found to date comes from the sporting world: the *Yale Dictionary of Quotations* includes an extract from the *Dallas Morning News* from 10 March 1976, in which a director of the baseball team Texas Tech Red Raiders is reported to have bravely used the phrase during a particularly tight match for his team: 'The opera ain't over till the fat lady sings'. Operas of course frequently involve a well-endowed soprano closing the proceedings with a famous aria, and so the connection with the idiom is a very plausible one. That said, the etymologist Michael Quinion quotes a 1976 booklet of *Southern Quotes and Sayings* that gives other forms to the saying, including 'Church ain't over till the fat lady sings'. If, as seems likely, the phrase had been around for some time before being recorded in print, it may have related to something entirely different, and have been part of Southern American slang for many years before.

The band Vampire Weekend has recorded a song called 'Oxford Comma'. I've always wondered what the **Oxford comma** really is. 44

The lead singer of Vampire Weekend, Ezra Koenig, has said that his song is more about life than a particular point of grammar, although his lyrics were apparently inspired by spotting a group on the social networking site Facebook called 'Students for the Preservation of the Oxford Comma'.

The song did indeed inspire a renewed interest in this curious punctuation mark which in the course of its lifetime has divided educationalists and journalists and proved more controversial than the notorious split infinitive.

So what is it? The **Oxford comma**, otherwise known as the 'serial comma', is an optional comma added before the word 'and' at the end of a list. So 'We ate steak, green beans, and sautéed potatoes' includes an Oxford comma; without it the sentence would still make perfect sense and the punctuation mark is largely a matter of taste. In other cases, however, the comma is needed to avoid ambiguity, as in 'The curtains come in black and white, red and yellow, and blue and green.' For many though, who were brought up to believe that a comma before 'and' is always wrong, the instinct is hard-set and even this last sentence would have them demurring.

For the record, the split infinitive is now largely accepted in modern texts although some grammarians retain a strong dislike of it. If it all began with *Star Trek*'s 'to boldly go', it now goes largely unnoticed and other debates have taken its place.

Curiously, Vampire Weekend's lyrics don't include any example of this contentious punctuation mark. Then again, the first line probably says it all: 'Who gives a f*** about the Oxford comma?' Some people certainly do.

The Birds and the Bees

Does being **ostracized** have anything to do with the behaviour of ostriches?

45

It's a nice idea, but the two words are in fact quite separate. **Ostrich** comes from an Old French word *ostruce*, dating right back to the twelfth century. The Latin term for the bird was *struthiocamelus*, meaning a 'sparrow camel', a word coined after the first encounters with ostriches, probably because of the animal's long neck. Eventually *struthio* stood on its own and was converted from French into the 'ostrich' we know today. **Ostracize**, meanwhile, has a very different history, and a colourful one too.

To ostracize someone is to exclude them from a community. The word comes from the Greek term *ostrakon*, the literal meaning of which was 'broken pottery'. In Athens and other ancient Greek cities, a citizen whose power or influence was considered dangerous to the state was sent into exile for five or more years. Any candidate for such banishment was the subject of a democratic vote. Each person eligible to vote would write down the name of the candidate they saw fit for banishment on a fragment of broken pottery or potsherd. The pieces were then counted, and if the votes deemed it popular, the person would be 'ostracized'.

Why do we call false sentiment **crocodile tears**? Can crocodiles really cry?

46

To shed **crocodile tears** is to put on an insincere act of being sad. The expression is very old, dating back to the mid-sixteenth century. An account of the life of Edmund Grindal, the sixteenth-century Archbishop of Canterbury, quotes him as saying, 'I begin to fear, lest his humility . . . be a counterfeit humility, and his tears crocodile tears.' It stems from the ancient belief that crocodiles, in order to lure their prey, would weep. The unsuspecting prey would come close, only to be caught and rapidly devoured, again with a show of tears. The crocodile's reputation for weeping is recorded as early as 1400, as in this quotation from the *Oxford English Dictionary* from a travel narrative: 'In that contre . . . ben gret plentee of Cokadrilles . . . Theise Serpentes slen men, and thei eten hem wepynge' (roughly translated as 'In that country . . . are plenty of crocodiles. These serpents slay men, and then eat them weeping').

But can a crocodile really weep? The experts say yes: they have tear glands just like most other animals. And zoologists have recorded alligators, close relatives of crocodiles, shedding tears while they're eating. This parallel may be significant—rather than being an emotional response, the shedding of tears probably happens because of the way crocodiles and alligators eat: when eating their prey they will often huff and hiss as they blow out air, and their tear glands may empty at the same time.

The idea of crocodile tears being false was used both in Edmund Spenser's *The Faerie Queene* and in Shakespeare's *Othello*. They provide just two of the many allusions in literature that have cemented the idiom in the language.

Incidentally, the word 'crocodile' means, literally, 'worm of the stones'. It is from Greek, and is a reference to the croc's habit of basking in the sun on the shingly banks of a river.

Why are houses built around an open space or alleyway known as **mews**?

I n 1066, the Normans arrived in Britain with an alien tongue and imposed it upon everything they encountered. Over the next three hundred years, as many as 10,000 French words came into English.

The supremacy of French was unstoppable, particularly in those areas that the nobility called its own. As Melvyn Bragg in *The Adventure of English* highlights, falconry, one pursuit of the aristocracy, gave us a whole host of words that have survived until the present day. A **leash** was once the strip of material used to secure the falcon, a **block** was specifically the platform upon which the bird stood. A **codger** is probably related to **cadger**, the (often elderly) man who assisted the falconer by carrying the birds in a cage, while the first **lure** was a leather device used to train the hawk. To **mew** was to moult, as falcons do: if a bird was 'in mew' it was confined to a cage during its moulting period. The cages in which falcons were kept were subsequently known as **mews**.

The Mews was also the name the former royal stables kept at Charing Cross in London, so called because they were built on the site of the royal hawk housing. Today's Royal Mews, near Buckingham Palace, got their name from the now figurative use of 'mews' for a group of stables or accommodation buildings built around an open yard.

Where does the expression **buy a pig in a poke** come from?

This idiom, which warns shoppers to inspect something carefully before buying it, goes back a remarkably long way. The first recorded instance of its use is from 1530s' London, where it is part of advice given to traders: 'When ye proffer the pigge, open the poke'. The *Oxford English Dictionary* carries a citation from 1583 that gives the following gloomy piece of advice: 'He is a foole, they say, that will buy ye pig in the poke: or wed a wife without trial'.

The unfamiliar element here is **poke**. This was an Anglo-Norman word that meant a bag. English adopted its diminutive form *poket* as 'pocket'. The idea behind the pig and poke proverb is that, if you are to avoid buying something that proves worthless, you must look in the bag before you buy—a more colourful version of the Latin tag *caveat emptor*.

In the phrase 'under the auspices of', what are **auspices**?

The root of **auspices** and the more familiar adjective **auspicious** are closely linked. If something is auspicious it bodes well, giving promise of a favourable outcome. In Roman times, people tried to predict future events by watching the behaviour of birds and animals. An *auspex* (Latin) was a person who observed the flight of birds, and viewed their behaviour as an omen of what might pass and, crucially, about the best path to take in important matters. The birds whose flight patterns were thought especially significant were generally eagles and vultures, while the *auspex* would also listen to the calls of others, such as owls, ravens, crows, and chickens. The historian Pliny wrote that the call of ravens was the worst cry of all, like a 'whine, as though they were being strangled'. Owls, meanwhile, were considered funereal, because they inhabited the night and 'inaccessible and awesome' places. The word *auspex* literally means 'a watcher or observer of birds', if not quite in the twitching sense we know today, and *auspicium* came to mean 'a premonition or forecast, especially of a happy future'.

If the ancient Roman *auspex*'s predictions were favourable, he was seen as the protector of the enterprise that was to be undertaken, and that is where we get the phrase **under the auspices of**, meaning 'with the support of' or 'under the patronage of'.

An *auspex* was also known as an *augur*, with the Latin *avis*, 'bird', once again at the probable root of the word, together with the Latin verb *garrire* meaning 'to talk'. Today, if something augurs well, it promises to have a good outcome.

Finally, *avis* is also the root of 'aviation', alluding to the flight of birds, and 'inauguration' too: something was inaugurated—consecrated or installed—after the omens taken from the flights of birds deemed it favourable.

Where does the idea of a **white elephant** come from?

To accuse something of being a **white elephant** is to label it a burden to those who possess it. The story of its origin is a distant and colourful one. Back in the days when Thailand was known as Siam, white elephants were highly prized animals. Whenever one was found it was automatically given to the king. Not only that, but it was considered a serious crime to neglect or mistreat a white elephant; in fact, even riding it was an offence. As a result, the maintenance of these rare animals was extremely expensive, especially as they couldn't be put to work of any kind. The wily king, whenever faced with an especially obnoxious courtier, would give the unsuspecting subject a white elephant as a special royal 'gift'. Such a present could, naturally, not be refused, and the care for the animal would usually ruin its new owner financially.

The phrase found its way onto English shores in the mid-eighteenth century after the Empire builders brought it home with them. It turned out to be particularly useful idiom for describing extravagant but highly impractical public buildings.

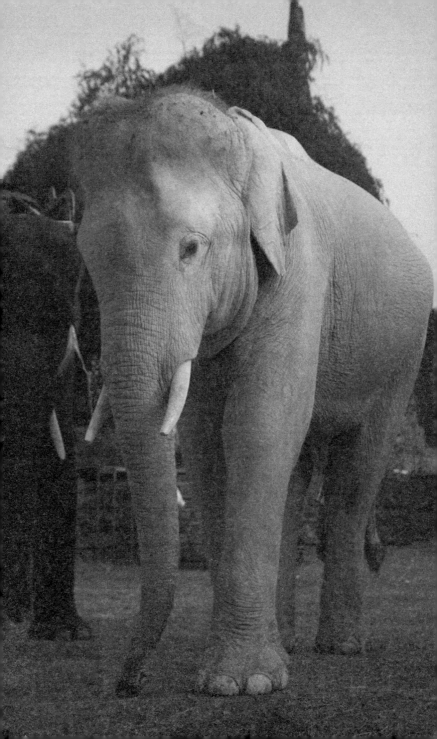

Is it true that the word **tragedy** originally meant 'goat-song'? And if so, why?

It is absolutely true. Many theories have been offered to explain it. One is that Greek tragedies were known as goat-songs because the prize in Athenian play competitions was a live goat. The contests were part of worship to Dionysus, involving chants and dances in his honour. The Romans knew Dionysus later as Bacchus, god of all things 'bacchanalian': in other words he freed people from their normal self through madness, wine, and ecstasy.

Sometimes the goat would be sacrificed, and a goat lament sung as the sacrifice was made. Hence the goat-song became intertwined with the Greek plays.

Others believe that in the plays themselves men and women would wear goat-costumes to dress up as satyrs—half-goat beings that worshipped and surrounded Dionysus in his revelry.

But by far my favourite suggestion is one that was offered in the *Guardian*'s celebrated *Notes & Queries* section. In answer to why the word **tragedy** comes from a word for goat-song, a Mr Marcus Roome of Clapton in London wrote simply: 'Have you ever heard a goat sing?'.

Who decides on the right collective noun for something?

The short answer is no one. While some languages, such as Spanish, French, and German, are ruled by committee there is no academy or governing body that decides on how English should evolve.

Indeed English has never been under the administrative rule of a language academy. A keeper of English, according to the eighteenth-century English grammarian and theologian Joseph Priestley, 'would be unsuitable to the genius of a free nation'.

Today's lexicographers are describers of English rather than lawmakers. The definitions they write are based on evidence from thousands of collected texts—newspapers, scholarly journals, teen magazines, text messages—and from transcriptions of the spoken word. This evidence is known in the trade as a 'corpus', and most modern dictionary publishers use one. Oxford University Press, the publishers of the *Oxford English Dictionary* and a range of current English dictionaries, holds a corpus of over one billion words of real twenty-first century English.

English, then, evolves with its own momentum. Collective nouns are no exception to the rule: many have been with us for centuries, while new versions of the old are emerging all the time, as well as completely new ones when a need arises.

The first collective nouns were typically ones for groups of animals and birds. A **parliament of rooks**, a **murmuration of starlings**, and an **unkindness of ravens** can each be traced back as far as the fifteenth century.

The etymologist Michael Quinion has noted that the first collection (not the official term) of collective nouns in English is *The Book of St Albans*, printed in 1486 in three parts on the subjects of hawking, hunting, and heraldry. In the sixteenth century, the book was apparently reprinted many times over, which kept the lists of birds and beasts in the public consciousness, and indeed many of the nouns are still in circulation today. Not all however: as Quinion notes, some strike a colourful chord but have never quite caught on, including a **fall of woodcocks** and a **shrewdness of apes**.

Back to the present day, and newly tried collective nouns include the tongue-in-cheek **stack of librarians** and a **groove of DJs**. No ruling body will decide upon their survival: that, like all new coinages, will be the decision of English's vast number of users.

Why are we **over the moon** when we're really happy?

Over the moon is a very old expression that dates right back to the seventeenth century. The *Oxford English Dictionary*'s first example of it is from 1718 and an extract from a play in which a character exclaims: 'I shall jump over the Moon for Joy!'. It was probably already a common expression when the nursery rhyme of around 1765 was first recorded: 'High diddle, diddle, The Cat and the Fiddle, The Cow jump'd over the Moon.' (The 'High' was later altered to 'Hey'.)

Amazingly, both the phrase and the nursery rhyme that popularized the expression have endured for almost 300 years with very little alteration. 'Over the moon' (together with 'sick as a parrot') has become part of the stereotypical patois of football players and commentators.

The moon features in quite a few other English idioms. To 'moon' over someone or something is to daydream or think longingly about them, as though one were gazing into space or at the moon. To 'moon' as in drop one's trousers probably came about because of the white shape of half-exposed buttocks!

Why is something that is the very best known as **the bee's knees**?

This curious expression is one of many similar sayings for something that is the acme of excellence. We are all familiar with **the cat's whiskers** (or **the cat's pyjamas**, **the cat's meow**, and **the cat's nuts**), which originated in the roaring 1920s and which might well have been the first of its kind—it is said to have originated from the name of the adjustable wire of the early radio crystal sets. But, while that phrase may have endured into the twenty-first century, many expressions born in the same decade of the flappers and bright young things have, sadly, long since faded from view. Clearly this

along with **bee's knees** there was a whole range of idioms describing 'excellence', most of them based on various parts of animals' anatomy and other attributes. They include *the canary's tusks, the flea's eyebrows, the bullfrog's beard, the cuckoo's chin, the kipper's knickers, the caterpillar's kimono*, and, my own favourite, *the elephant's adenoids*.

All of these expressions rely upon a jesting touch of nonsense with a bit of alliteration thrown in. They are precursors of the now familiar **the dog's bollocks**, which according to the slang collector Eric Partridge was originally a printing term for a colon followed by a dash.

'The bee's knees', curiously for an expression that evolved to mean 'the very best', first described something insignificant or very small; in the late 1800s there was a popular Irish expression **as weak as a bee's knees**.

The humble bee has been the source of many other British expressions, including **having a bee in one's bonnet** (an eccentric whim or craze on some point) and **making a beeline** for something: a straight line between two points on the earth's surface, such as a bee was supposed to take instinctively in returning to its hive.

The **spelling bee**, meanwhile, a party assembled to compete in the spelling of words, is just one kind of gathering: in the US a bee is a meeting of neighbours to unite their labours for the benefit of one of their number, such as when farmers unite to get in each other's harvests in succession. There are also apple-bees, husking-bees, quilting-bees, barn-raising bees, and even, in the early 1900s, public lynching bees. The word was chosen because of the social nature of the insect.

Questions of English

I am terrified of **clowns**. Is there a word for it?

The term is **coulrophobia** and is said to be suffered by many, including Johnny Depp. The first part '*coulro—*' was borrowed from a Greek word meaning 'stilt-walker', as clowns weren't known in the classical world. The second part '*—phobia*', meaning an extreme or irrational fear or dislike, is a highly productive suffix. Whilst most of us are familiar with **agoraphobia** (a fear of open spaces) and **xenophobia** (a dislike of foreigners), there are some formations that are that little bit more surprising (sometimes for good reason):

acrophobia: a fear of heights
ailurophobia: a fear of cats
neophobia: a fear of the new or unfamiliar
arachibutyrophobia: a fear of peanut butter sticking to the roof of your mouth
batrachophobia: a fear of frogs
mycophobia: a fear of mushrooms
deipnophobia: a fear of dinner parties
ergophobia: a fear of work
thalassophobia: a fear of the sea
laliophobia: a fear of talking or of stuttering when talking
gelophobia: a fear of laughing
hippophobia: a fear of horses
logophobia: a fear of words

erythrophobia: intolerance of the colour red
lepidophobia: a fear of butterflies
symmetrophobia: a dread of symmetry
triskaidekaphobia: a fear of the number 13

During coverage of the Olympics I heard several commentators use **medal** as a verb. Surely this is wrong as well as ugly?

56

This particular instance of 'verbing' got a lot of people going. The turning of a noun into a verb has always been unpopular—even Keats was criticized for writing in one poem of turtles that 'passion their voices'. Yet we use the end results of this linguistic process all the time: when we 'text' a friend, 'mentor' a colleague, 'rollerblade' in Hyde Park, or 'tough' something out.

Medalling probably came under particularly heavy criticism because, to the ear, it is indistinguishable from 'meddling'. Critics denounced it as part of a highly irritating modern trend that must be stopped. It may be a surprise to learn, however, that it has been around in this exact sense of 'winning a medal' since 1966, and came into real currency during the Barcelona Olympics of 1992. Ugly it may be, but perhaps not as much as the verb 'to podium', which was also used on more than one occasion in Beijing. London in 2012 may see some linguistic as well as sporting challenges.

Do lexicographers ever make mistakes?

Oh yes! In general phrases that move away from their original incarnation and become 'wrong' by themselves (of which my favourite is 'hammer and thongs' instead of 'hammer and tongs') are simply described by dictionary writers, whose job it is to describe what they see and hear, not what they would like to be the case. But editorial mistakes certainly can, and do, happen, and there is one very famous example to prove it.

One of the most notorious lexicographical errors of the twentieth century was the appearance of the word **dord**, which appeared in the second edition of *Webster's New International Dictionary* in 1934. The term was listed, on page 771, as a noun meaning 'density' in the fields of physics and chemistry, and there it remained for five years before the error was spotted. What error? The mistake was due to the erroneous filing of an index card (then the preferred system of collecting words) for an abbreviation, which simply stated 'D or d: density'. As the editor-in-chief of the dictionary wrote years later: 'As soon as someone else entered the pronunciation, "dord" was given the slap on the back that sent breath into its being'. While the word has now sadly been removed from *Webster's dictionary*, it continued to reappear for several years afterwards in other dictionaries that used *Webster's* as a source.

How did **Cockney rhyming slang** originate?

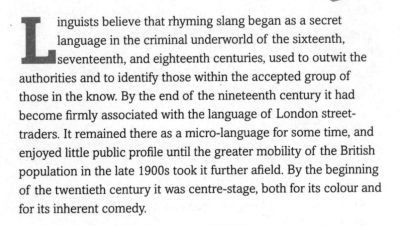

inguists believe that rhyming slang began as a secret language in the criminal underworld of the sixteenth, seventeenth, and eighteenth centuries, used to outwit the authorities and to identify those within the accepted group of those in the know. By the end of the nineteenth century it had become firmly associated with the language of London street-traders. It remained there as a micro-language for some time, and enjoyed little public profile until the greater mobility of the British population in the late 1900s took it further afield. By the beginning of the twentieth century it was centre-stage, both for its colour and for its inherent comedy.

The exact development of the term **Cockney** has proved elusive, for it has made many leaps of meaning over its lifetime. Originally, in the fourteenth century, it was a 'cock's egg' (with 'cock' being a male chicken, and *ey* being a Middle English word for an egg). There is, of course, no such thing, as male chickens don't lay eggs: the term was in fact referring to a misshapen hen's egg that was of little use. At some point in the Middle Ages a 'cockney' was the term used for a spoilt child, over-indulged by its mother—the connection with the misshapen egg was perhaps with the idea of the runt of a litter needing extra care. By the 1700s a cockney was a town-dweller, thought to enjoy an easy life when compared to the hardship of rural folk. It is only at the start of the eighteenth century that the first records emerge of the use of 'Cockney' to mean someone from London, and then of course someone very specifically born in the City of London within the sound of Bow Bells.

Much of the rhyming slang we use today is from its earliest days—'trouble and strife' (= wife), 'apples and pears' (= stairs), 'Adam and Eve' (= believe), and they are almost always used for humorous effect. But far from dying out or living in the past, this category of slang is thriving in parts of the world, and in particular Australia. The latest British incarnations are **Mockney** and **Popney**; the first describing the language of those affecting a Cockney accent, and the second a whole new lexicon based on the names of celebrities. So we might have a 'Steffi' (Steffi Graf = laugh) over a couple of 'Britneys' (Britney Spears = beers), regret everything 'going Pete Tong' (= wrong), put on some 'Billy Ocean' (= suntan lotion), or spot the 'Jerry Springers' (= mingers). Love it or hate it, rhyming slang is alive and well.

How many words are there in English?

Language is first and foremost a spoken medium—fewer than a thousand of the world's 6,800 languages have writing systems—and as such the number of words it contains and produces at any one moment is infinite. Dictionaries of current English can only hope to provide a snapshot of a language at a given time. There is as a result no definitive answer to this question, and that's perhaps as it should be, given the fluidity and unpredictability of English itself. The *Oxford English Dictionary*, a permanent record of the language—once a word is in, it stays in—

has approximately 600,000 words and derivatives of those words, but it is necessarily very far from exhaustive, for words need to prove themselves before they can earn a place.

In 2009 there was a lot of attention given to the claim that English was about to reach its millionth word (the chosen one, 'Web 2.0', had been around for some time). A news-grabbing claim, certainly, but an unlikely one. English probably exceeded a million words some years ago. The main problem in trying to quantify its vocabulary is how to agree the basics: what is a word? Do you include terms such as 'text' that can mean a multitude of things, can be a verb and a noun, and that has numerous spin-off forms such as 'texter', 'texting', 'text-walking', etc.? And how about obsolete words, or highly specialized and scientific ones?

What does seem likely is that English has more words than other comparable world languages. Throughout its history it has been exposed to an enormous number of influences—German, Dutch, Norman French, Hindi, and Latin, to name just a few. It continues to hoover up foreign words and has shown itself to be readily adaptable to different cultures across the world. The rate with which global 'Englishes' are being developed suggests that the size of the language is set to expand still further rather than diminish.

Why do some words have two opposite meanings? And what are they called?

ingle words that have two contradictory meanings are known as **contranyms**, although the term itself has yet to make it into a dictionary. The number of contranyms in English is small, but they are significant. Examples include:

dust: **1** to remove dust. **2** to cover with dust.
hysterical: **1** frightened and out of control. **2** funny.
nervy: **1** showing nerve or courage. **2** excitable and volatile.
moot: **1** debatable. **2** not worth debating.
fast: **1** moving quickly. **2** solid and unable to move.
seed: **1** to sow seeds. **2** to remove seeds.
weather: **1** to withstand a storm. **2** to wear away.
screen: **1** to show, e.g. a film. **2** to hide something.
bound: **1** fastened to a spot. **2** heading for somewhere.
sanction: **1** to approve something. **2** to boycott something.
apology: **1** an expression of regret for something. **2** a defence or justification of something.
strike: **1** to hit. **2** to miss (in baseball).

Terms like these are also sometimes called **Janus words**, named after an ancient Italian deity, regarded as the doorkeeper of heaven and represented as having two faces, one on the back and one on the front of his head. Janus words look both ways thanks to their contradictory meanings. (Incidentally, the month of January is also named after Janus, as it stands at the entrance of the new year.)

Words such as those listed above take on different meanings purely as a result of usage over time. The word **blunt** began to mean 'dull' or 'obtuse' in the context of a knife right at the end of the fourteenth century; 100 years later it could also mean 'sharp' in the context of a direct and unceremoniously made comment. Similarly, to **bolt** something is to fix it firmly, but can equally be applied to someone springing away with a sudden bound. Both meanings, separated by some 300 years, emerged from the original use of 'bolt' to mean a projectile or missile such as an arrow: it could travel at great speed and was also shaped like a pin that could be used to fasten something down.

Another in the same category came about through changes in pronunciation. The word **cleave** can be used for 'splitting apart' or 'joining together'. Etymology reveals that Old English had two words: *cleofian*, 'to stick together', and *cleofan*, 'to split apart'. Over time the two words began to sound the same and merged into one word, 'cleave'.

Does a double negative a[lways] mean a positive? And can a double positive make a nega[tive?]

What a complicated question. Unfortunately the answer is no less tricky.

To start with the double negative: there are several kinds. George Orwell thought that the category found for example in 'her behaviour was not unkind', i.e. 'not' followed by a negative adjective and normally used with an intentional cancelling effect, should be 'laughed out of existence'. Another type, illustrated in such sentences as 'I never doubted you wouldn't make it', was denounced in *Fowler's Modern English Usage* (a book viewed by many as the classic authority on grammar and style and written back in 1926, although updated since) as a 'fuzzy error'.

But it is the double negative found in such sentences as 'I don't take no money from him' or 'He never did no harm to no one' that arouses the strongest passions and which is frequently among the top ten of native English speakers' bugbears.

It would probably then surprise many of us to learn that double negatives were once a perfectly standard feature of English, found in writers as illustrious as Chaucer, Shakespeare, and many others right up until the seventeenth century. Over time, however, the mathematical principle replaced the linguistic one, and two negatives (just like two minuses in maths) began to indicate a positive. From then on in, the double negative became a way for indicate a lower-class person 'of vulgar tongue', and by ... nineteenth century its use was roundly condemned.

What the double negative 'rules' don't take into account, however, are the subtleties of English that we draw on all the time. 'That's not strictly untrue', like the 'not unkind' example above, reflects our need for more than black and white distinctions. The real world is full of such in-between gradations of meaning. 'Not untrue' implies much more caution than simply 'true', and suggests a shade of doubt about the veracity of the statement in question.

As for George Orwell's objection, he found that the 'not unkind' type of double negative allows people to sit on the fence too often, coming down on neither the positive side nor the negative. His suggested cure for people who used this kind of formulation was to memorize the sentence 'A not unblack dog was chasing a not unsmall rabbit across a not ungreen field'. That is fine as far as it goes, but Orwell was being uncharacteristically unsubtle about the intentionally grey areas of the language he so adored.

Of course, hedging your bets with the double negative can make you easy prey for lampooning. Jenny Cheshire, in an excellent article in a collection called *Language Myths* about the claim that double negatives are always illogical, quotes from 'The Secret Diaries of John Major' in the satirical magazine *Private Eye*, published at the time when Major was PM. It goes:

'Monday
I was not inconsiderably sorry to see all the news placards this morning. They all had in very big letters NEW TORY SEX SCANDAL.

Wednesday
I do not know whether to be very not inconsiderably annoyed or

quite not inconsiderably pleased. This morning I saw on the hotel's CNN News that no sooner have I turned my back than the great economic recovery has come to an end. This only goes to show how wrong I was to leave Mr Heseltine in charge.'

Finally, there is the question of whether the principle works in reverse: i.e. can two positives make a negative? The answer is no, neither in maths nor in language.

Yeah, right.

What is the strangest change in meaning that any word has undergone?

I can only give a very subjective answer, but I'll start with a few nominations.

Most of the words in everyday English have been in (and occasionally out of) circulation for centuries. A study of them in a historical dictionary such as the *Oxford English Dictionary*, which charts chronologically the story of a word from its birth to the present day, can reveal startling changes in meaning. A **pedant** was in the sixteenth century a schoolmaster, while the *OED* gives 'strong and vigorous' as one of the earliest meanings of **nervous** (as in full of nerves, or sinews). There are many other such examples. **Promiscuous** used to mean confused or undistinguished, while the first **punk**, in the sixteenth century, was a prostitute.

A **chaperone** was so called in allusion to the *chaperon*, a hood or cap formerly worn by nobles. One 1864 writer put it like this: 'Chaperon . . . when used metaphorically means that the experienced married woman shelters the youthful *débutante* as a hood shelters the face.' Perhaps the chaperone would protect against **muggers**, although the original muggers were sellers of mugs, i.e. earthenware. (The use of 'mug' to mean the face probably came about because of drinking mugs made to represent a grotesque human face which were so common in the eighteenth century.)

To call someone a **bully** was, in the sixteenth century, to effectively say 'good fellow' or 'darling': it was a term of endearment that could be used to either sex. It was only in the seventeenth century that this mate became someone who showed off his good deeds, and a century later the intimidating tyrant of the weak.

The word **nice**, derived from Latin *nescius* meaning 'ignorant', began life in the fourteenth century as a term for 'foolish' or 'silly'. From there it embraced many a negative quality, including wantonness, extravagance, and ostentation, as well as cowardice and sloth. In the Middle Ages it took on the more neutral attributes of shyness and reserve. It was society's admiration of such qualities in the eighteenth century that brought on the more positively charged meanings of 'nice' that had been vying for a place for much of the word's history, and the values of respectability and virtue began to take over. Such positive associations remain today, when the main meaning of 'nice' is 'pleasant' (if with a hint of damning with faint praise; it may yet turn full circle).

Teenage slang is a highly productive generator of new meanings for old words. The motivation for such subversion is similar to that for any code: it excludes those people outside the circle and confers membership on those within it. Words of approval are often bad turned good, including the now familiar **bad**, **wicked**, **savage**, **bitchin'**, and, more recently, **sick** and **shabby**.

My two favourites, though, have to be **assassin** and **aftermath**. Although disputed by some, the origin of **assassin** was probably the Arabic word for 'hashish-eater'. At the time of the Crusades, it is said that fanatical warriors were sent forth by their sheikh, the 'Old Man of the Mountains,' to murder the Christian leaders. One text of around 1860 explains: 'The assassins, who are otherwise called the People of the Man of the Mountain, before they attacked an enemy, would intoxicate themselves with a powder made of hemp-leaves, out of which they prepared an inebriating electuary, called hashish.'

As for **aftermath**, that word, right up until the nineteenth century, was used for the new grass that grew after mowing or harvest. A *math* was a mowing of the grass, and *mathday* was the mowing day.

How did the **exclamation mark** and **question mark** signs come about?

Both these punctuation marks were originally manuscript abbreviations in Latin texts.

To take the **exclamation mark** first: it derives from a vertical version, written in the margins, of the Latin word *Io*, meaning 'exclamation of joy'. The vertical stroke was the 'I' above the 'o', in which the 'o' eventually became a dot.

The **question mark**, meanwhile, goes back to the word *Quaestio* meaning 'questioning, investigation' and indicating a question. *Quaestio* was eventually abbreviated to a curly 'q' above the 'o', while the 'o' became a dot.

Why were these marks needed in the first place? Their prime function in Latin manuscripts was to show people the right intonation: a question, a surprise, a shout, etc. If you combine them you get a different effect: ?! delivers an immediate sense of incredulity: a little like smileys or emoticons in our text messages today.

What is the most useless word in the English language?

A far more frequent question is 'What is the best word in the English language?' (see **serendipity**, p. 51), any answer to which is of course subjective, just as any candidates for the most redundant word would be (**redundant**, by the way, is formed from two Latin words, *re* meaning 'again', and *undare* 'to surge' (from *unda* 'wave'): in other words, something that overflows and so is excessive).

One exchange in the regular *Notes & Queries* column in the *Guardian* debated the most useless word in the English language. A respondent from Canterbury offered the following, all taken from the *Chambers English Dictionary*:

wayzgooze: an annual picnic for members of the printing profession.

stillicide: the right to drop water on someone else's property.

corsned: the practice of establishing someone's guilt or innocence by seeing whether they are able to swallow a large piece of mouldy cheese.

Another reader decided to try to top these, and offered instead:

taghairm: divination, especially the inspiration sought by lying in a bullock's hide behind a waterfall.

My own candidates are:

any word ending in **–age**. Since the *Buffy the Vampire Slayer* TV series, which experimented with language to great effect, the '–age' suffix has been added liberally to almost any word of the speaker's choosing. The words **bronzage** (self-tanning), **webbage** (web-based content), and **spendage** (expenditure) are particular offenders in my book.

winningest (and its opposite, **losingest**): an American term for 'the best', 'most attractive', or 'having the most wins', depending on context.

quillow: a recent blend for a pillow that folds out into a quilt (**guyliner**, eyeliner for men, is a close second).

grubhood: the condition of being a grub.

Do **meritorious** and **meretricious** mean the same thing?

These two words, neither of which trips off the tongue, have quite different origins and mean very different things.

To start with the simpler **meritorious**, it means 'deserving of merit or praise'. It is now largely used within theological contexts where it means 'entitling a person to a reward from God'.

This sense of the word, which dates right back to the twelfth century, is however distinct from an earlier Latin word *meritorius* which meant 'hired', and which survived with reference especially to prostitution. And therein lies the link with **meretricious**, and the possible confusion between the two.

'Meretricious' comes from a very similar Latin term, *meretrix*, which also meant a prostitute. The *Oxford English Dictionary*'s first citation of the term is from Francis Bacon in 1626, who wrote the provocative line 'The Delight in Meretricious Embracements, (wher sinne is turned into Art) maketh Marriage a dull thing'.

From there it took on the more figurative meaning of 'alluring by false show; showily or superficially attractive but having in reality no value or integrity'.

There is a lovely story about the (correct) use of the word 'meretricious' which involves the writer and social critic Gore Vidal. The British writer Richard Adams, appearing alongside Vidal on the satirical TV comedy show *That Was The Week That Was*, called his work 'meretricious'. 'Pardon?' said Vidal. 'Meretricious,' repeated Adams. 'Meretricious to you,' the American replied, 'and a happy new year'.

Is **snuck** the right past tense of **sneak** or should it be **sneaked**? 66

ood question. The grammarian's term for a verb that forms its past tense by adding '-ed' or '-t' to its stem, as in 'walked', 'cooked', or 'burnt', is a 'weak' verb. A 'strong' verb (a term invented by the folklorist and grammarian Jacob Grimm) on the other hand, changes the vowel within the stem, so 'take' becomes 'took' in the past tense, 'steal' becomes 'stole', and 'break' becomes 'broke', etc. (There is another category of verbs, those that have completely irregular forms or conjugations, such as 'went' for 'go'.)

As for **sneak** and **snuck**, the following extract from *The New Fowler's Modern Usage* (1998) explains:

'From the beginning, and still in standard British English, the past tense and past participle forms are *sneaked*. Just as mysteriously, in a little more than a century, a new past tense form, *snuck*, has crept and then rushed out of dialectal use in America, first into the areas of use that lexicographers label 'jocular' or 'uneducated', and more recently, has reached the point where it is a virtual rival of *sneaked* in many parts of the English-speaking world. But not in Britain, where it is unmistakably taken to be a jocular or non-standard form'.

Interestingly, new verbs coined today are almost always weak— **texted**, **googled**, and **blogged** are three examples. In the past, there were far more strong verbs than today. In Anglo-Saxon times there were said to be as many as 300, while today fewer than 100 survive. Many have changed over from strong to weak, as in **glide** whose past form used to be 'glad', 'glode', or 'glid' but which changed over at a time of large change during the Middle English period.

There are some verbs in addition to 'sneak' that still confuse today as they hover between being 'strong' and 'weak'. The past tense of the verb **dive**, a century ago, was 'dove' rather than 'dived' as it later became. Today, however, and particularly in American sources, 'dove' is making a comeback.

Other verbs, particularly those made up of two words, can also cause problems. Is it 'troubleshot' or 'troubleshooted'? (Both are in circulation at the moment and so, given that language is a democratic enterprise, both can hold their own.)

In some cases, of course, a weak and a strong past tense of a verb co-exist because they mean very different things. So 'a man was hanged this morning' is correct, but a picture would be 'hung'.

Which is right, **realize** or **realise**?

The short (and probably for many, unsatisfactory) answer is both. There isn't really a hard rule about the suffix **-ize/-ise**. British spelling has always recognized the two variants, but when American spelling was standardized during the nineteenth century, mainly through the efforts of the pre-eminent American lexicographer Noah Webster, the use of '-ize' was one of the conventions that became established as the norm.

Since then, the '-ise' ending for verbs such as 'realise' has become progressively more popular in Britain and in other English-speaking countries such as Australia, perhaps as a reaction against the American custom and a desire to be distinct. Spellings such as 'organisation' would at one time have struck many older British writers as rather strange and foreign-looking. The *Oxford English Dictionary*, however, favours '-ize', partly on the linguistic basis that the ending derives from the Greek suffix *-izo*. This was also the style of *Encyclopaedia Britannica* (even before it was American-owned) and, until recently, of *The Times* newspaper.

So far the decision to '-ise' or '-ize' has been largely a matter of taste. There is however one definite advantage of the modern '-ise' habit, which is that it removes any confusion over a handful of important words that should not be spelt with '-ize'. These include words that happen to end in '-ise' but which have nothing to do with the Greek root at all. Among these are words that end in '-vise', such as **televise** or **supervise**, words that end with '-cise' (as in **circumcise** or **exercise**), and terms that end in '-prise' (as in **comprise** and **apprise**).

If we are all supposed to be so rude nowadays, why do we still need so many euphemisms?

Even a permissive society needs to soften a linguistic blow sometimes. For no matter how liberal, or how accepting we become, the power to offend is always there. What changes are the subjects that cause that offence.

Firstly though, what is a euphemism? The flamboyant actor and writer Quentin Crisp once remarked that 'euphemisms are unpleasant truths wearing diplomatic cologne'. His description captures perfectly the role of euphemistic expression: it is a means of verbally sidestepping something unpleasant by giving it another name. It is a hugely useful and versatile device, for it can deliver humour, kindness, irony, or sarcasm according to what we need.

The subjects which invite euphemism vary according to our times and preoccupations. If the Victorians baulked at prostitution, childbirth, and bankruptcy, today there are new subjects requiring sensitivity, such as ethnicity and race. Some, however, such as sex, drink and drugs, madness and death, have remained remarkably constant throughout hundreds of years.

Mental illness has been the subject of euphemism for centuries. It still is. A **lunatic**, as early as the thirteenth century, was someone whose madness was believed to have been dependent upon changes of the moon (*luna* is Latin for moon). Some six hundred years later, **doolally tap** became a slang term for 'mad' in the British army. The expression originated in India and the military sanatorium at Deolali, north-east of Bombay, which also doubled as a transit-camp where soldiers would await their boat home at the end of their duty tour. As boats only left between November and March, some soldiers were there for many months, during which boredom set in and behaviour began to deteriorate. Men became, in fact, 'doolally tap': 'doolally' being the Englishman's pronunciation of Deolali, and 'tap' being an Urdu word for 'malarial fever'. The men, in other words, had 'camp fever'.

Moving on, if someone is **round the bend**, they are a successor to those who dwelled in Victorian hospitals, where mentally unsound patients were confined to areas invisible from the end of the typically long and splendid hospital driveways. Today's euphemisms for madness are often injected with black humour, as in variations on the formula **three cards short of a full deck**, **one bit short of a byte**, and **one French fry short of a Happy Meal**. To be **Upminster**, meanwhile, is to be completely mad, so chosen because the town is a few stops past **Barking** (a euphemism which draws on canine behaviour) on the London tube map. Comic relief is a useful defence against unpleasantness or fear.

In the world of business management, euphemism is a useful tool, albeit for many an unwelcome one. Over the course of the last 170 years, to **be fired** (itself a euphemism, perhaps from the image of a gun being discharged) has, variously, been termed **sacked** (having been given a sack into which to pack one's personal belongings), **laid off**, **given the air**, **made redundant**, **let go**, and **deselected**.

The need for euphemism remains, it seems, as robust as ever.

Riddles and Fiddles

What is the longest word in English?

The longest word in current use is **deinstitutionalization**, which has 22 letters. There are however many other words of comparable length that are either nonce-creations or in technical use and so are not encountered very often. The following are to be found in the *Oxford English Dictionary*:

immunoelectrophoretically	(25 letters)
psychophysicotherapeutics	(25 letters)
thyroparathyroidectomized	(25 letters)
pneumoencephalographically	(26 letters)
radioimmunoelectrophoresis	(26 letters)
psychoneuroendocrinological	(27 letters)
antidisestablishmentarianism	(28 letters)
floccinaucinihilipilification	(29 letters)

Pneumonoultramicroscopicsilicovolcanoconiosis
(45 letters) has for years been the popular vote as the longest word in English. It is in fact an artificial coinage dating from 1935, designed to make it into the record books, which it certainly did. James Joyce made up nine 101-letter words in his novel *Finnegans Wake*, the most famous of which is **Bababadalgharaghtakamminarronnkonnbronntonnerronntuonnthunntrovarrhounawnskawntoohoohoordenenthurnuk**, a coinage apparently designed to reflect the symbolic thunderclap that

accompanied the fall of Adam and Eve. Joyce's fictional word is not generally counted in the longest word stakes given that it was never (unsurprisingly!) picked up for further use. **Supercalifragilisticexpialidocious**, the 34-letter title of a song from *Mary Poppins*, is in several dictionaries but again has not lost its original very specific and fictional associations.

The longest words containing no letter more than once are currently **uncopyrightable** and **dermatoglyphics** (the study of skin markings on hands, fingers, and feet).

Why is **lisp** so hard to say if you have one?

An excellent question, and one of many similar ones, including 'Why is **abbreviation** such a long word?', 'Why is the use of over-long words called **sesquipedalian**?', 'Why isn't **palindrome** the same spelt backwards?', and 'Why does **monosyllabic** have five syllables?'

Frustratingly, there are no satisfying answers to any of them, except that English users have perhaps been over-logical and under-creative. 'Abbreviation' comes from the Latin *ad* (to) and *breviare* (to shorten), while 'sesquipedalian' was taken, in the seventeenth century, from a phrase used by the Roman lyric poet Horace—*sesquipedalia verba*—meaning 'words a foot and a half long'. Perhaps Horace's tongue was firmly in his cheek. 'Palindrome' is a simple and direct translation of a Greek word that meant 'running back'. A **semordnilap**, meanwhile, has become a term in its own right for a word or phrase that makes sense when read backwards, but which crucially is not the same as the original: so *desserts* and *stressed*, *diaper* and *repaid*, *decaf* and *faced*, and *deliver* and *reviled* are all semordnilap pairs.

Finally, to the question of **lisp** vs. **lithp**: frustratingly for all lispers the word is an evolution of a very old word indeed—*wlisp* from Old English. In almost 1,000 years no one has come up with a more sympathetic alternative.

What is the synonym for a **thesaurus**?

There seems, ironically, not to be one! The word **thesaurus** comes from a Greek term meaning a treasure house, and indeed the modern thesaurus is seen as a storehouse of information. The usual definition is 'a book that lists words in groups of synonyms and related concepts', which is hardly pithy.

Clearly we need a synonym for 'thesaurus'. And a collective noun for a pile of thesauri while we're at it?

Why do we still **dial** a phone when the technology is now very different?

There are actually quite a few linguistic leftovers of this kind. In most cases the versatility of English ensures that a word simply adapts to its new environment and shifts its meaning accordingly. In Samuel Johnson's eighteenth-century dictionary, a **pet** denoted a lamb taken into a house and reared by hand: over time it broadened out to mean any domestic animal. **Meat**, for the Anglo-Saxons, was a broad term for food: as variety of diet increased, so it acquired the specific meaning it has today.

Technology, however, works a little differently, probably because words are highly specific in their meaning. As a result, as technology moves on, even the most successful new word can become defunct, as was the case with **squarials**—the proprietary name for a type of diamond-shaped dish aerial for receiving satellite television broadcasts in the late 1980s, which never quite took off.

If the word 'squarial' disappeared as soon as the objects did, there are many examples of words where the original technology has long since gone, but where language has simply stayed still. As well as **dialling a number**, we also talk about **hanging up** at the end of a phone call, or of a phone being **off the hook**. In a hotel we expect fresh **bed linen**, even though the bedclothes are mostly made of cotton. We still **roll down** our car window even though the need to do so in newer cars is no longer there.

We **type** a letter to our bank manager, **paste** information onto a document, and **scroll** down a computer **page**. We tape a **movie** that has been **filmed**, or **record** news **footage**—even when today the technology is almost entirely electronic.

We still speak about **telegraph poles** even though the telegraph has been dead for over a century. And some of us own a **penknife** with no pen, sticking with the name for a utensil that goes all the way back to the fifteenth century when it was a small knife used to make and mend quill pens.

There isn't as yet an official name for such words, although one term used has been 'skeuomorph': a label from architecture and archaeology for an object that retains design elements which were necessarily present in the original but which are now entirely ornamental.

Other languages have such leftovers too: one linguist's blog points out the Japanese word 土木学, which today means civil engineering but which, character-by-character, reads as 'earth-wood-study'.

There are apparently three words that end with **-gry**. **Hungry** and **angry** are two of them. Which is the third word in the English language?

73

This question is not what it appears to be. It seems in fact to have begun as a trick question, and the riddle has been circulating in email for some years, in various forms, having appeared in print media before that. The answer is in fact 'language' (the third word in the phrase 'the English language').

There are however a number of other English words ending in **-gry** and which are listed in the *Oxford English Dictionary*. Some are extensions of the word **hungry** itself, so **overhungry** and **unhungry** are sometimes found in modern sources. Other, more exotic terms which would be considered rarities are **aggry**, meaning an African bead, **iggry**, an old army slang term meaning 'hurry up', **skugry**, a sixteenth-century word meaning 'secrecy', and **meagry**, a now obsolete term meaning 'meagre-looking'.

Are there cases of **Chinese whispers** in language, when words change as they are passed on and stay that way?

Oral 'mis-transmission'—whereby words change as they are passed on verbally and their new form moves towards becoming the norm—can be a subtle and slow process and the results are sometimes hard to detect. Indeed, some of our most common idioms and grammatical constructions are, the result of linguistic Chinese whispers.

to have another thing coming: the idiom was originally *to have another think coming*, which dates from 1937. The use of *thing* is now however extremely well established, as in this line from the popular sitcom *Only Fools & Horses* in 1999: 'If you think I'm staying in a lead-lined Nissan hut with you and Grandad and a chemical bloody khazi you've got another thing coming.'

bog standard: instead of *box standard*. The term means basic, unmodified, or unexceptional; the original *box standard* is said to have applied to motorcycles that were brand new and unmodified, 'straight out of the box'.

should of: instead of *should have*. Similarly **could of**, **would of**, etc. The use *of* simply represents the unstressed pronunciation of *have*, and is often used humorously. However, it is also becoming increasingly common in some regional dialects and in speech:

'A Metropolitan Police spokesman said that he suspected Miss Nightingale, 70, may of ate a bun and that there might of been all jam on her mouth when the wasp struck.' (*Viz* comic, 1999)

arse over tit: instead of *arse over tip*. This phrase has the equivalent meaning of 'head over heels'. The mutation of *tip*, used in the sense of the utmost part of the body, into *tit* seems to have taken place around the late 1960s, and probably resulted simply from the logical equation of two slang terms for parts of the body.

off one's own back: instead of *off one's own bat* (meaning doing something on one's own initiative).

to hone in on something: instead of *to home in on something*. The use of *hone* is frequently considered a typographic error, misunderstanding, or phonetic alteration of *home*.
However, it has become sufficiently widespread, especially in US English, to be considered a sense in its own right.

to tie you over: instead of *to tide you over*. The idea behind the original phrase, which is first recorded in around 1860, is of a swelling tide that will carry you over an obstacle in your path. It is used particularly in relation to money.

to curry favour: instead of *to curry favel*. *Favel* was the name of a horse in a medieval French romance, which became a symbol of cunning and duplicity. To 'curry' or 'rub down' Favel was to use cunning. Over time, the allusion was lost and 'favour' made better sense.

If you can be **disgruntled**, can you be 'gruntled' too?

There are some words in English that, as they are largely negative, seem likely to have a positive partner in another word. **Disgruntled** is a perfect example: why can't we be **gruntled** when things are going well, and could we ever have been in the past?

'Gruntle' has actually never been a word with particularly positive associations. It is essentially a diminutive form of 'grunt', and was originally used in reference to pigs rather than people. A 'gruntler' was an occasional term for a grumbler, but the adjective 'gruntled' has never come to be taken seriously and is almost always used to humorous effect, as in this sentence by P.G. Wodehouse who relished new coinages: 'He spoke with a certain what-is-it in his voice, and I could see that, if not actually being disgruntled, he was far from being gruntled' (*The Code of the Woosters*, 1938).

There are other examples of unpaired words of this kind. We can no longer be (and in some cases never could be) **ruly**, **kempt**, **consolate**, **couth**, **shevelled**, **chalant**, or **ept** unless we are using the words as deliberate nonsense opposites for comedy value. Some of these words did exist at some point in English's past but have faded from view. **Couth** was once a word meaning 'affable, agreeable' and has survived in the Scottish dialect word **couthie**; **ruly**, meanwhile, died out in the fifteenth century but did for a time mean 'law-abiding' and 'orderly'. **Dishevelled**, on the other hand, came over from a French word *déchevelé*, which described messy hair. **Shevelled** was never a word that caught on.

It is curious that it is largely the negative forms of words that have survived where the positive existed. We may, for example, be **impecunious**, **untoward**, and **unwieldy**, but no longer their opposite. 'Untoward', for example, is formed from a now obsolete medieval sense of 'toward' that meant 'obliging' or 'docile'. If someone was 'wieldy', meanwhile, they were capable of wielding a weapon.

The opposite trend, whereby it is only the positive that remains, is much harder to find.

Just how many words are there for a remote control?

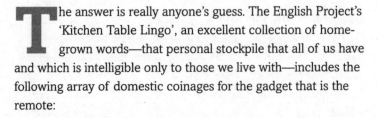

The answer is really anyone's guess. The English Project's 'Kitchen Table Lingo', an excellent collection of home-grown words—that personal stockpile that all of us have and which is intelligible only to those we live with—includes the following array of domestic coinages for the gadget that is the remote:

bimmer, blapper, blitter, blooper-dooper, boggler, bomper, bumper, buttonbox, butts, cajunka, channel changer, channel-panel, clicky,

commander, conch, dibber, digotrondit, dobar, doflicka, donker,
doobery, doofer, dooty, flicker, flipperdopper, flugel, hoofer-doofer,
kadumpher, oofadoofa, phaser, pilot, pinger, plinker, podger, presser,
pringer, rees-mogg, splonker, spurgler, tinky-toot, turner-upper,
twanger, twidger, wanger, widger, wiz-wiz, woojit.

There are apparently dozens more. Why this word attracts quite
so many possibilities is a mystery, although 'remote control' hardly
trips off the tongue.

Sailors were the first people to talk about **gadgets**. The word
started out in nautical slang as a general term for any small device
or mechanism or any part of a ship. The first recorded use is from
1886, from a rookie sailor's diary: 'Then the names of all the other
things on board a ship! I don't know half of them yet; even the
sailors forget at times, and if the exact name of anything they want
happens to slip from their memory, they call it a chicken-fixing,
or a gadjet, or a gill-guy, or a timmey-noggy, or a wim-wom.' The
word is probably from the French word *gagée* meaning a tool.

Then there is the **widget**, first recorded in the 1920s in the USA,
in the sense of a small gadget. It's probably just a fanciful variation
on 'gadget', and of course in the 1990s a widget became a specific
sort of device used in some beer cans to introduce nitrogen into
the beer and to give it a frothy head.

A **gizmo** and **doofah** are other names we give a remote control.
No one knows the origin of 'gizmo', alas, but a doofah probably
comes from the idea of 'that'll do for now'. A **doodah**, meanwhile,
comes from a refrain of a plantation song sung by slaves on the
Southern plantations of America.

What was the first ever **Knock Knock** joke?

William Shakespeare has over 14,000 quotations in the *Oxford English Dictionary*, a greater number than any author, living or dead, and more than the Bible, the second most prolific source of new words and idioms. Even in the knowledge of Shakespeare's productivity, however, it needs some stretch of the imagination to put him at the beginning of today's infinite collection of **Knock Knock** jokes. But a reading of *Macbeth* will convince you otherwise.

The scene in which the all-important dialogue occurs (Act II, scene 3) involves a porter who is slightly the worse the wear from the previous night. He hears a knocking, and muses out loud about how, were he the gatekeeper of hell, he would be kept very busy. With each repeated knock at the door (from Macduff, as we later discover), the Porter recounts various fictional characters who might come knocking: first a farmer who hanged himself because of poor financial prospects; then an 'equivocator', one who speaks with ambiguity to avoid speaking the truth; and finally a tailor who stealthily steals cloth by making his customers' trousers too small.

This motley crew of characters would have resonated with Shakespeare's audiences, drawn as they were from real practices of the day. The Porter's joke breaks the tension building with the discovery of blood on Macbeth and Lady Macbeth's hands. More

importantly in answer to this question, however, is that each fictional character that the Porter imagines being behind the door is greeted with a shouted 'Knock, knock! Who's there?'. And so the scene was set for thousands of 'Knock Knock' jokes ever after.

Urban Myths and
Folk Origins

My Spanish friend tells me that **avocado** used to mean a lawyer in her language. How did two such different things end up with the same name?

78

When we hear a new word, especially one that has come over from a foreign language, we often deal with it by changing it to something more familiar. **Avocado** is a perfect example of folk etymology. The avocado pear originated in tropical America, and took its name from the Nahuatl language of central Mexico. The local name was *ahuacatl*, which meant 'testicle' and which was chosen because of the fruit's shape.

The Spanish conquerors of the sixteenth century, when they took Central America, returned with many indigenous words, including *ahuacatl* which they changed slightly to the less unpronounceable *aguate*. This must still have sounded strange to Spanish speakers, however, because before long they substituted a similar-sounding Spanish word—*avocado*, which did indeed mean, literally, a lawyer and which shares the same root as the English 'advocate'.

The strange story doesn't end there however. When English speakers discovered the delights of the avocado they found that word clumsy and unfamiliar. Their replacement? 'Alligator pear', which was the name for the next 200 years and which only finally died out when twentieth-century cuisine put the pear-shaped fruit firmly on the linguistic map.

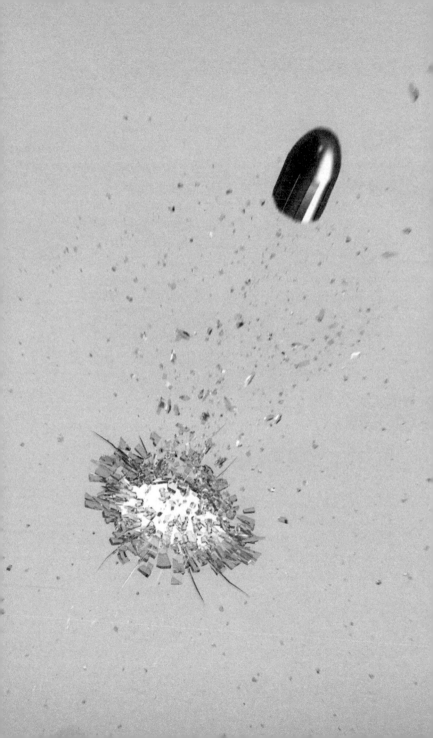

Was a **parting shot** once a real bullet?

79

A **parting shot**, a phrase used to mean a final remark, usually pointed or cutting, made by a person at the moment of leaving, started out as something quite different: a 'Parthian shot'. And it was indeed both live and dangerous.

The Parthians were an ancient race living in southwest Asia; they were skilled warriors with exceptionally clever battle tactics. Parthian horsemen would baffle their enemies with their rapid manoeuvres; most deadly was their strategy of discharging missiles backwards while fleeing or pretending to flee. A Parthian shot was, quite literally, a lethal one.

The idea of delivering this final blow passed figuratively into the language in the seventeenth century. Over time 'Parthian' was corrupted to 'parting' as fewer people understood the allusion—and, of course, the replacement makes perfect sense.

There is another wonderful phrase, much less used, which also describes a parting comment, but with a crucial difference: it is a comment thought up by a person leaving a situation and which would have been the perfect retort had it come to mind at the time. **Esprit de l'escalier**, French for 'wit of the staircase' and coined by the eighteenth-century philosopher Diderot, brilliantly sums up that frustration of thinking of exactly the right response to someone as you are on your way out, when the opportunity to make it has gone.

Why are **spare ribs** 'spare' in the first place?

The first part of **spare ribs** actually has nothing to do with the English sense of 'spare'. The term started off, many centuries ago, in northern Germany, where the term was *ribbesper* (the anglicized 'ribspare' is still found in some very local English dialects), which consisted of pickled pork ribs roasted on an open spit.

When English speakers began to relish this German dish, some time in the sixteenth century, they changed the name to something that sounded more familiar, and so 'spare ribs' were born. It might just as easily have become 'spear-ribs', for the old German *sper*, meaning 'spit', is related to the English word 'spear'.

Does history record the very first **forlorn hope** and **lost cause**?

It does, and the result might surprise you. To take **lost cause** first, this is now a phrase so entrenched in everyday English that few of us would wonder if it were anything other than a general term for a mission or project that is highly unlikely to succeed. But it was, and once had a very specific application following the American Civil War.

The term 'Lost Cause' first appeared in the title of a book published in 1866 by the historian Edward A. Pollard, and was later cemented by a number of articles written for the Southern Historical Society. The Lost Cause became a recognized term for an intellectual movement that aimed to reconcile those from the American South with their defeat in the Civil War and, crucially, to console them with the idea that their loss was due to blind aggression, betrayal and incompetence rather than any just cause or military skill.

At the turn of the twentieth century Mark Twain was still referring to the Lost Cause as this specific loss, and indeed the term (when capitalized) has retained much of that resonance today for some Americans. The shift to a general sense was gradual but assured, and by the 1910s the figurative meaning co-existed happily alongside the specific one.

As for **forlorn hope**, the original version was not what you might believe. This example of folk etymology began as a Dutch term *verloren hoop*, 'lost troop'. It originally referred to a band of soldiers sent ahead as the vanguard of an attack ('vanguard' has the same root as *avant-garde*, i.e. something that goes ahead of the rest). The *verloren hoop* was inevitably far more vulnerable to attack, and so was often lost in battle.

For English speakers, the word 'forlorn' was already there to make sense of the Dutch term and to bring it firmly into their own language. 'Forlorn' comes from Old English *forloren* which meant 'morally corrupted', with the core idea being 'lost'. This sense of 'lost' or 'pitifully sad' took over in the sixteenth century, and so a ready-made English version was there and waiting for the lost troops of the Netherlands and their fateful missions.

In the word **nickname**, what does the 'nick' mean?

82

Nickname is a good example of how spoken English holds sway over the written form. Before the printing press, language was a strictly oral business. An *eke-name* was an additional name given to someone (*eke* meant a supplement or add-on), but the 'an' and 'eke', barely distinguishable when spoken, were gradually blended together to produce 'nick'. By the same process, a *nadder*, a *noumpere*, and a *napron* became an 'adder', 'umpire', and 'apron' respectively. A *noumpere*, incidentally, meant literally a 'non-peer': someone who is set apart from the other players.

Why is a helpmate or friend called a **mucker** in my home town of West Bromwich?

83

The very first meanings of **mucker** were literal ones: first recorded in the thirteenth century, it referred to a cleaner of stables who removed dung and could also denote a person who prepared soil for planting. In the early 1800s it started to be used to describe someone who bungled things and who was therefore incompetent. This sense of contempt was strengthened when 'mucker' took on, in the nineteenth century and in the US, the sense of a troublesome or rowdy person. It also, in American university slang, denoted a 'townie'.

In the mid-1900s, though, 'mucker' took on positive connotations, first within British military circles and then more widely. It denoted a close companion or friend, with whom one regularly socialized or indeed 'mucked in', which originally meant to share rations. It is often used as a form of address—the *Oxford English Dictionary*'s first quotation is 'What's the griff [news], mucker?', from a military novel set in the Second World War.

Today, 'mucker' is still used for a friend or mate, particularly in the Black Country including of course West Bromwich.

The questioner mentions the word **helpmate**: that too is an interesting term, as it's the result of a misunderstanding made as long ago as the seventeenth century. The first mention of 'helpmeet' is in the King James Bible, where God, referring to Adam, says 'I will make him an helpe meet for him' (this help was to be Eve). In this sentence from Genesis (2:18), 'meet' is used as an adjective meaning 'suitable' or 'appropriate'. A few decades later the poet Dryden was writing that 'if ever woman was a help-meet for a man, my Spouse is so', thus providing the *OED* with its first record of the use of 'helpmeet' as a noun. From there it was a relatively simple step to 'helpmate', which of course makes every sense, and so the modern term was born.

Expletive Deleted

My mother would often mutter '**sweet Fanny Adams**' when she meant 'nothing at all'. Isn't that rude?

This expression was certainly popular among the wartime generation and it wasn't considered to be particularly rude at the time. Fanny Adams was a real person, the child victim of a gruesome murder that took place in 1867, committed by a solicitor's clerk named Frederick Baker who butchered her body and distributed it over a wide area of Hampshire. Before long, and with a good helping of black humour, Royal Navy sailors were using her name as slang for tinned meat or stew.

The modern development of the meaning 'nothing' is unrelated to these macabre beginnings. It was probably influenced by the initials F.A. which are used as a euphemism for 'f*** all': 'sweet Fanny Adams' means essentially the same thing.

Did **Gordon Bennett** as an exclamation ever make it into the dictionary?

It certainly did. The *Oxford English Dictionary*'s first record of Mr Bennett's name being used to express surprise, incredulity, or exasperation is 1937, and it is still to be found in the speech of the older generations.

The story of the real Gordon Bennett is now a familiar one: a Scottish-born journalist, James Gordon Bennett Jr was the son of a newspaper mogul who became famous for conducting the first ever modern newspaper interview, covering the murder of a prostitute in 1836. Gordon Bennett Jr took over the *New York Herald* from his father but was apparently more interested in good living (including lavish mansions and yachts) than in keeping up the circulation that his father had worked to achieve. Bennett's flamboyant lifestyle and drunken escapades apparently scandalized New York society, and it is this reputation that is said to have inspired the exclamation of disbelief at each account of his latest antics.

The one hitch with this story is that the date in which the exclamation **Gordon Bennett** is said to have entered the language is considerably later than the activities of the phrase's real namesake. The link remains frustratingly elusive, and it is entirely possible that the name was simply taken because it sounded similar to 'Gorblimey', 'God', or 'Gawd' and was therefore a useful euphemistic substitute.

We shall probably never know. But that won't deter word sleuths from the hunt.

I remember **flaming Nora** and **flipping Ada** being the expletives of choice in my childhood. Who were Nora and Ada and why were they singled out for attack?

86

There is a very neat theory that **flaming Nora** is the result of the Cockney pronunciation of 'flaming horror', with 'flaming' being an established euphemism, particularly in the north of England, since 1922: it is first recorded in one of D.H. Lawrence's short stories. The theory of the Cockney origin makes good sense but falls down, sadly, for lack of proof. Some of the best stories about word origins are apocryphal, but they are often the most fun to relate.

The earliest pieces of evidence for 'bloody Nora', which is how it all seems to have begun, are from Bill Naughton's 1957 novel *One Small Boy* and the television sitcom *Nearest and Dearest* from the late 1960s. Both of these place the term firmly in Lancashire. Examples of 'flamin'' and 'bleedin'' appear later and as euphemisms for 'bloody'. But why Nora? Clearly the name is working as a euphemism for 'hell'—like 'eck', and the best guess is that it was simply a characteristic local name (the later 'Nora Batty' would show a similar choice). There is a history in twentieth-century slang of adopting typical personal names as terms (see *I'm A Celebrity (Get Me In the Dictionary)*, p.137). Other examples include 'Nancy' to mean an effeminate man and 'Molly', which used to be a byword for a prostitute. 'Mary Ellen' was used for a working-class woman or market trader in Liverpool at around the same time that 'bloody Nora' appeared.

Flipping Ada follows exactly the same pattern: 'flipping' being a euphemism for 'f***ing' since 1911 (again, interestingly, the first citation is from D.H. Lawrence, this time from his novel *The White Peacock*). Ada, like Nora, was a very popular Christian name in the 1940s and 50s.

Is **bloody** really still a swear word?

In 1916, George Bernard Shaw's Eliza Doolittle, heroine of his play *Pygmalion*, shocked the rest of the cast (and the theatre audience) with her 'Walk! Not bloody likely. I am going in a taxi'. To the explanation that it is 'the new small talk', one character says sadly, 'I shall never be able to bring myself to use that word'. Almost a century later, in a public relations coup for Australia, the British advertising regulator banned an ad by the

Australian Tourist Board. The Australians had, it announced, done everything to make their country the perfect holiday destination: the camels had been shampooed, the tree ferns fertilized, the Tasmanian devils pacified. In spite of these and other preparations in place, the hosts were still waiting. 'So,' the tagline ran, 'where the bloody hell are you?'.

Bloody was traditionally seen as highly offensive. Much of this was down to the false etymologies ascribed to it, and in particular the belief that it derived from blasphemous oaths such as 'God's blood' or 'by Our Lady'. In fact, the term is a reference to 'bloods', a seventeenth-century label for aristocrats who were the hell-raisers of their time. 'Bloody drunk' was another way of saying 'as drunk as a blood'.

Some swear words, over time, become diluted in their capacity to shock, and so it has proved with 'bloody'. Prince Charles's whispered comment to his sons about journalists—'bloody people'—inadvertently picked up on a microphone during a Royal press shoot, caused a furore because of the Prince's attitude rather than his ripe language: his use of the 'B-word', as it was once known, merited scarcely a mention. In Australia too, as the ad showed, 'bloody' is far from being an expletive, but rather a word conveying an open, unstuffy hospitality. (Then again it was the Australians who even twenty years ago felt safe to say they 'wouldn't give a XXXX for anything else' but Castlemaine lager.)

If 'bloody' is now too tame to describe today's aristocratic rowdies, when it comes to swearing we mostly keep to the old. The fact that we encounter **f*****, for example, with such frequency seems to have shaken little of the power it has held for over 500 years. In spite of appearances, our taboos seem to be surprisingly secure.

I once heard George Bush used the term **cojones**. Does that make it official enough to put it in the dictionary?

George W. Bush did allegedly use this term, the Spanish word for 'testicles' used in the same way as 'balls' when referring to courage or 'guts'. Bob Woodward, in his book *Plan of Attack*, noted that Bush told the former Labour Communications Director Alastair Campbell that 'your man has got cojones' after Tony Blair had pledged British troops to the war effort in Iraq in 2004. Bush assumed that his joke would be understood by his team alone, for he is said to have added 'of course, these Brits don't know what cojones are'.

Bush was wrong. **Cojones** is indeed in the dictionary, but not just current ones. Even if Bush's use did bring it back into the spotlight, it had already been in the *Oxford English Dictionary* for some time. The word has been around at least since the 1930s —the *OED*'s first citation is from Ernest Hemingway's *Death in the Afternoon* in relation to the role of violence in sport (notably the book's theme of bullfighting): 'It takes more cojones to be a sportsman where death is a closer party to the game.'

'Cojones' is still considered to be pretty high on the offence register in Spain (the equivalent, perhaps, of the English 'bollocks'). Perhaps its foreignness dilutes its impact over here—certainly if an American president feels free to use it the rest of us might feel entitled to do the same.

Were **cripes** and **crikey** ever rude?

These two exclamations are today so mild that they scarcely qualify as expletives at all. But that is what they once were, being euphemisms for 'Christ!'

The *Oxford English Dictionary*'s first record of **cripes** is from a 1910 novel and in the form of 'By cripes!' **Crikey**, too, has its roots in a religious phrase—or rather in its avoidance. Like 'cripes', it is a softening of 'Christ' and goes back even further, to the 1830s.

Gadzooks is another in the list of old-fashioned exclamations that are more at home in the *Beano* and *Billy Bunter* than today's list of profanities. That word is usually said to be an alteration of 'God's hooks', that is, the nails by which Christ was fastened to the cross. In fact, there's a whole list of oaths from the late seventeenth and early eighteenth centuries that used 'gad' as a thinly disguised version of God, among them *Gadsbobs*, *Gadsniggers*, *Gadsbudlikins* (a corruption of 'God's body' or 'bodikins'), *Gadsprecious*, and *Gadswookers*.

Maybe we should bring them back in.

I'm A Celebrity
(Get Me In the Dictionary)

Who was the first **Smart Alec**?

English is littered with phrases that use a person's name as shorthand for a particular type of person or character attribute. **Clever Dick**, **Contrary Mary**, and **Billy No Mates** (see p. 153) are all examples of names that were never (as far as we know, and save for nursery rhymes) attached to a single and original person.

You'd be forgiven for thinking that **Smart Alec** fits into this category too. Traced as far back to 1865, the phrase is used generically to mean a know-it-all who is just a bit too smug about his self-confessed intellectual superiority. For years linguists have believed that 'Smart Alec' was simply the close relative of 'Clever Dick'. In the mid-1980s, however, Gerald Cohen, in his *Studies of Slang*, put forward a convincing argument that the Alec in question was in fact an Alex, and a celebrated thief in New York in the 1840s.

The man in question, Alexander Hoag, apparently worked in tandem with his prostitute wife Melinda and an accomplice who went by the colourful name of French Jack. Together they formed a formidable team that would fleece unsuspecting visitors to the city and then share the loot with two police officers, who were in on the racket and who gave them protection from any charges in return.

The etymologist Michael Quinion has uncovered an account by George Wilkes, the assistant editor of a New York periodical *The*

Subterranean, which describes one of the many ruses practised by Hoag's gang. While in prison for libel in the infamous New York prison called The Tombs, Wilkes met Hoag and heard all about his exploits. Wilkes, an outspoken critic of police corruption, described the trick in a diary of 1844, *The Mysteries of the Tombs*. He wrote: 'Melinda would make her victim lay his clothes, as he took them off, upon a chair at the head of the bed near the secret panel, and then take him to her arms and closely draw the curtains of the bed. As soon as everything was right and the dupe not likely to heed outside noises, the traitress would give a cough, and the faithful Aleck would slily enter, rifle the pockets of every farthing or valuable thing, and finally disappear as mysteriously as he entered.' Hoag would then make the customer scarper by banging loudly on the door in the guise of a cuckolded husband.

Hoag's ambition was also his nemesis, however. He tried to cheat his police accomplices out of their share by various means, including lying in wait behind a wall over which Melinda would drop the loot without the officers' knowledge. Thanks to exploits such as these it was only a matter of time before Melinda and Alec were arrested.

Gerald Cohen's guess is that 'Smart Alec' (with Alec being a shortening of Alexander), was coined by the police as a nickname for anyone who outsmarts themselves—in this case by thinking themselves cleverer than the authorities. Whether or not this is apocryphal is impossible to say, but, if true, it would be a neat ending to an entertaining story.

Why is the letter no man wants to receive known as a **Dear John letter**?

A **Dear John letter** is one in which a woman tells her boyfriend or husband that she wishes to end their relationship. It is definitely American in origin: the first quotation in the *Oxford English Dictionary* is from an issue of the *Democrat & Chronicle* from 1945, in which it is clearly referenced as RAF slang.

'"Dear John,"' the letter began. "I have found someone else whom I think the world of. I think the only way out is for us to get a divorce," it said. They usually began like that, those letters that told of infidelity on the part of the wives of servicemen . . . The men called them "Dear Johns"'.

But why John? The probable answer is that John was a common generic name for a man at this period—the term **John Doe**, for example, was common legal jargon for an unknown plaintiff in a legal action as well as a name for an unidentified corpse or patient in a hospital. In fact the *OED* lists over twenty uses of 'John' prefixed to another word to form a name or nickname with a specific sense, including **John Citizen**, **John Trot** (a bumpkin), **John Thomas** (a livery servant, and also the penis), and **John Hancock** (a signature). As for the 'Dear . . .', any serviceman receiving a letter from his wife or girlfriend that began with that stiff form of address would know at once that bad news was coming.

Most of us have written or had an experience of a Dear John letter at some point. The modern female equivalent, much less known, is a 'Dear Jeannie' letter.

Why do the Americans call Britons **Limeys** and **Poms**?

I n the 1850s, a newly-arrived British immigrant in Australia was known as a *lime-juicer*. For some years before, the term had been applied to British sailors on Navy ships for whom the drinking of lime juice was compulsory, thanks to its high vitamin C content that protected against the disease scurvy (or rickets) that had been rife on the high seas.

'Lime-juicer' was abbreviated to **Limey**, and was soon applied to any Briton, sea-faring or not. The nickname has kept its resonance for Australians ever since.

The other, even more popular, term for Britons in Australia is **Pom**. There have been many wonderful guesses at its origins spanning many decades, including the acronyms 'Prisoner of Her Majesty' (which was stamped on the clothing and equipment worn by British convicts) and 'Permit of Migration'. Other colourful possibilities advanced to explain 'Pom' are the Navy's nickname for Portsmouth, 'Pompey', from where emigrants to Australia set sail, and even *pommes de terre*, as a nod towards the potatoes eaten in great quantities by British troops during the First World War.

After decades of colourful conjecturing we are now pretty close to the truth. For it, we need to look to rhyming slang, which as so often may be based on the name of a real-life character, in this case a Jimmy Grant. Frustratingly, that's all we know about

the man in question (possibly the name was chosen for being quintessentially English), but 'Jimmy Grant' was adopted, by workers on the wharves of Melbourne harbour, as the term for any immigrant in the early 1900s. Over time, 'Jimmy Grant' shifted to 'Pommy Grant', probably as a reference to the red-skinned 'pomegranate' and the easily-burned complexions of newly-arrived Britons on the Australian shores. Eventually, 'Pommy' or 'Pom' became a term on its own.

Why do we describe someone as being **as happy as Larry** when they are particularly content? Who was or is Larry?

93

The phrase **as happy as Larry** has been around in print since the early 1900s, but was probably a spoken idiom for many years before that. The Larry in question is thought to be Larry Foley, a renowned nineteenth-century Australian boxer who retired at 32 and collected a purse of £1,000 for his final fight, making him very happy indeed.

If this story seems a little far-fetched, there is another possibility which some etymological detectives prefer: the word **larry** in some parts of Britain once meant 'a state of excitement', and was common enough to be found in the novels of Thomas Hardy. A **larrikin**, meanwhile, also originated in Britain (notably in parts of

Warwickshire and Worcestershire) and meant a mischievous youth. Like so much local dialect, it travelled to Australia along with the early settlers and became there the home equivalent of a hoodlum or rowdy. Perhaps larrikins, in a state of 'larry', were so carefree and mischievous that they inspired the modern phrase. We shall probably never quite know for sure, and if that isn't enough, Samuel Beckett, the great playwright, added his own theory to the mix in his novel *Murphy*, and introduced a grimly humorous note in the process:

'The melancholic's melancholy, the manic's fits of fury, the paranoid's despair, were no doubt as little autonomous as the long fat face of a mute. Left in peace they would have been as happy as Larry, short for Lazarus, whose raising seemed to Murphy perhaps the one occasion on which the Messiah had overstepped the mark'.

Was there ever a **real McCoy**?

94

A s so often in cases like these, there are numerous contenders for the role of McCoy in this phrase, which has been with us since at least the 1850s.

Part of the problem facing researchers is that McCoy is a fairly common surname. Adding to the confusion is the fact that the earliest versions of the phrase give the saying as 'the real McKay': an 1856 example from the *Oxford English Dictionary* has it describing a brand of whiskey, made by the distillers G.

Mackay and Co. who used the tagline 'a drappie [drop] o' the real McKay' to advertise their product. 'The Real McKay' was the same distillers' advertising slogan in 1870 and this was certainly how Robert Louis Stevenson knew it when he used it in his writings as a current idiom to mean 'the real thing' or 'the genuine article'.

Now for the mysterious next step: how did McKay become McCoy? Thanks to the British love of whisky, 'the real McKay' was clearly in common currency by the end of the nineteenth century, but was this the ultimate origin of the phrase we still use today? Many believe not; the broadcaster Alistair Cooke recounted in one of his celebrated *Letters from America* that a famous American cattle baron called Joseph McCoy was the ultimate source of the saying: this McCoy, the story goes, promised his investors that he would bring 200,000 cattle from Texas to Chicago in the space of ten years. In the event he is said to have brought ten times as many in only four years.

Another claimant to the title of the real McCoy is one William S. McCoy, a smuggler of illicit liquor during the US prohibition era, who is said to have gone against the shady habit of rum-runners of the time of watering down their alcohol in order to maximize profits. William McCoy, by contrast, became famous for never watering his booze, and selling only real top-quality products. As a result, some have unsurprisingly placed him as the real Real. McCoy.

By far the likeliest reason for the McKay/McCoy switch lies elsewhere. Norman Selby, who fought under the sobriquet Charles 'Kid' McCoy, was an American boxer who became welterweight champion in 1896 after knocking out Tommy Ryan, his sparring partner, to whom he had made out he was both unpractised and unfit. Selby is said to have demonstrated such one-upmanship more than once, prompting commentators to wonder which was 'the real McCoy'. At the same time, Selby became so famous that he is said to have had many imitators who stole his name up and down the land. His response was to bill himself as Kid 'the real' McCoy from then on. With such a popular hero as this, the spelling change would have been complete.

Who or what is a 'tod' in the expression **on my tod**?

James Forman Todhunter Sloan was an American jockey. In the last decade of the nineteenth century he was the foremost rider in the thoroughbred racing circuit on the East Coast. He was the pioneer of a sitting position known as the 'monkey crouch' used by jockeys today.

In his day 'Tod' Sloan, as he was best known, was a major celebrity, thanks both to his passions for riding and to his flamboyant pursuit of the finer things in life. It was thanks to the latter that his career came to an unexpected end when he was suspected of betting on races in which he himself was competing. He was banned from racing in both Britain and America, and died an early and lonely death from cirrhosis of the liver. Tod Sloan was indeed alone, and this rhyming slang, together with the sad facts of his demise, is the basis for our saying **to be on one's tod**.

Where did the idea of the **devil's advocate** originate?

In medieval times, the **devil's advocate** (in Latin *advocatus diaboli*) was a canon lawyer within the ecclesiastical legal system of the Roman Catholic Church. The first to take on this role was appointed by Pope Sixtus V in 1587 to challenge any proposal to turn a dead person into a saint. The Pope's aim was to present a rounded picture of the person in question, including any negative aspects, in order to ensure that canonization was done in full knowledge of the candidate's history. The devil's advocate would take a sceptic's role and argue against the lawyer advocating sainthood.

Today, a devil's advocate is a person who argues the contrary side of any issue in order to give it fair play, and not because they necessarily believe that the negative should win the discussion.

Why do we call a small person a **titch**?

It is not often that a person can boast of getting his name in the dictionary. Delia Smith famously did so in 2002, when the phrase 'doing a Delia' meant putting on a feast based on the celebrated chef's recipes. And so did Harry Relph, many years before, although not quite as he might have expected.

Relph was a diminutive English music-hall artist in the late nineteenth and early twentieth centuries. He was famous for his various character roles, including The Gendarme and The Tax Collector, but was equally renowned for his height, or, at 4 feet 6 inches (1.37m), his lack of it. His most popular routine was known as the Big Boot dance and involved Relph dancing with a pair of 28-inch boots. All of this was done under Relph's stage name—'Little Tich'.

Relph had acquired his nickname as a child—not because of his height, as **titch** was not yet part of the language. Rather it was because of his apparent resemblance to a notorious figure of the day dubbed 'the Tichborne Claimant'—real name Arthur Orton. Orton, who had been working as a butcher in Wagga Wagga in New South Wales, had returned to England from Australia claiming to be none other than Roger Charles Tichborne, the heir to a very large fortune. Tichborne was thought to have been lost at sea but his mother had refused to believe that her son had perished, and spent many years sending enquiries across the world in an attempt to find him. One such enquiry found Orton, who turned out to bear very little resemblance to Charles Tichborne and who came unstuck during detailed questioning in court. Orton was convicted for perjury and sentenced to fourteen years' hard labour.

The Tichborne trial was notorious, lasting over 188 days. Such was the interest from the public that, when Relph used his nickname, no one would have doubted the associations. It is thanks to his small stature that the word 'tich' or 'titch' entered the language, however: the term was popularized by British soldiers during the First World War who applied the nickname to any small person.

In the phrase **Bob's your uncle**, who on earth is Bob?

The most popular theory about **Bob's your uncle** is that it comes from an act of political nepotism. It is said that the Prime Minister of the 1880s, Robert Cecil (Lord Salisbury), appointed his young and inexperienced nephew Arthur Balfour to a number of posts, including Chief Secretary for Ireland, in favour of others more eligible for the roles. This was said to have been less than well received by the electorate, who decided that if Bob was your uncle, then you could have pretty much everything in life. Alas, the dates to this nice story don't quite match the first appearances of 'Bob's your uncle'; most linguists today believe that the idiom goes back to the slang expression 'all is bob', meaning everything is fine and dandy.

I've heard that the original **peeping Tom** spied on Lady Godiva. Is that true?

Yes, it is—at least partly. Thomas, and its abbreviation Tom, has been a generic name for a male for over a thousand years. Other words and phrases featuring the name include **tomfool**, **tomboy**, **Tom Farthing** (a fool or simpleton), and **Tom, Dick, and Harry**. The latter phrase, meaning a large number of undistinguished people, comes from an eighteenth-century song that featured the line 'Farewell, Tom, Dick and Harry, Farewell, Moll, Nell, and Sue'.

The character of **Peeping Tom** appears in the well-known story of Lady Godiva, who according to legend rode naked through the streets of Coventry in protest against her own husband's oppressive taxation of the people. Lady Godiva, whose name is attested to in the Domesday Book, is said to have issued a public proclamation that all doors and windows be shut. Peeping Tom is the name given to a prying tailor who is said to have been struck blind (or, in some versions, struck dead) after defying the order and watching Lady Godiva secretly.

The 'partly' equivocation at the beginning of the answer comes from the fact that 'peeping Tom' first appears in the city accounts of Coventry in 1773, some 600 years after Lady Godiva is thought to have made her infamous journey. It was around this time too that the first mention of Godiva's hair protecting her modesty appears.

Incidentally, the belief that Peeping Tom was the first person to mutter the oath 'God blind me', the origin of 'Gorblimey' and 'blimey', is almost certainly unfounded. Those two mild expletives don't appear until the end of the nineteenth century.

I've heard that **the full monty** refers to Field Marshal Montgomery and his breakfast habits. Is this true?

It may be, but there are other more likely origins of the phrase, which means the equivalent of 'the full works' and which jumped right back into currency with Peter Cattaneo's 1997 film of the same name, in which a group of Sheffield steel-workers become strippers after being made redundant (thus giving another shade of meaning to **the full monty**).

To take the Montgomery story first: the suggestion is that the General (as he was during the Second World War), whose nickname was indeed 'Monty', used to insist on a full English breakfast each morning. Over time his name was taken up by ex-servicemen after the war and became the byword for 'the whole lot'. The trouble is that the expression 'the full monty' is only recorded in print (as far as Oxford's lexicographers can find) since the 1980s, although there is anecdotal evidence that it existed before then and that it was often applied to a full English breakfast and was also the name given to several fish and chip shops.

Other theories have been proposed too, including a link to the gambling term 'monte', referring to the stockpile of cards left after each player has had their share. In Australia, meanwhile, a Monty in a horse race is a horse that is a safe bet, while 'for a monty' means 'certainly, for sure', and some believe there is a link back to this much older term.

By far the most plausible story, however, is even more colourful. Montague Burton was a highly successful tailor (founder of the clothing empire that still bears his name) who produced made-to-measure suits in the early part of the twentieth century, having also contributed significantly to both World War efforts by producing uniforms for nearly a quarter of the armed forces. Burton's firm, in Chesterfield in Derbyshire, was said to offer both a two-piece suit as the standard and also a waistcoat and spare pair of trousers for an additional cost—thus, the theory goes, 'the full Montague Burton' meant the full set. The phrase was eventually shortened to 'the full Monty' and applied to the total or whole of anything.

While this is certainly the story with the most to substantiate it (the phrase seems to have been far more prevalent in the north, for example, where Burton's empire began), it is by no means proven beyond doubt. As with so many phrases, we may never know the whole truth.

There are other very similar phrases that may also spark curiosity, including **the whole kit and caboodle**, which like 'the full monty' means 'everything', 'the works'. This term was originally 'kit and boodle', with the 'ca' added on for alliteration. 'Boodle', in nineteenth-century America, was counterfeit money, particularly as used as a means of gang bribery and corruption. The connection between this and the phrase 'kit and caboodle' is puzzling but some linguists believe that the idea was of a bunch of money (the similar word 'buddle' used to mean a bundle) that, together with one's kit, prepared you for anything.

Who was **Billy No Mates** and did he know **Jack the Lad**?

101

As far as we know there was no single unfortunate **Billy No Mates**. The term originated in the early 1990s as a T-shirt slogan, and followed the pattern of many a name coined in those years such as the comedian Harry Enfield's 'Tim Nice But Dim' and 'Loadsamoney'. Unlike those two epithets, however, 'Billy No Mates' has passed so effortlessly into the language that the term has made it into the *Oxford English Dictionary*: it is defined as 'a person regarded as lonely or having no friends'. In other words, exactly what it says on the tin.

Jack the Lad has been around for a lot longer than 'Billy No Mates': 300 years, in fact. Legend has it that the original 'lad' was one Jack Sheppard, the 22-year-old son of an English carpenter born in London's Spitalfields in 1702. Thanks to his criminal exploits as a thief he became notorious, as well as much wanted by the authorities. The story goes that he was arrested and imprisoned four times but that, crucially, he managed each time to make a spectacular escape from St Giles' prison in spite, it is said, of being on one occasion both handcuffed and manacled to the floor.

Such daring ingenuity would clearly capture the public imagination—Sheppard became a wildly popular hero of the poorer classes. The *OED* includes an extract from a nautical ballad of 1840 which gives a flavour of the reputation of the character who had become the model for a Jack the Lad: 'For if ever fellow took delight in swigging, gigging, kissing, drinking, fighting, Damme I'll be bold to say that Jack's the lad.'

Jack Sheppard was finally hanged on the gallows at Tyburn, witnessed, it is said, by 200,000 people. His body now lies in the churchyard of St Martin's-in-the-Fields. Whether or not he was the inspiration for today's 'Jack the Lad' may never be completely clear, but his story certainly lives on in legend if not in language.

Index